Contents

The youth
Diverging path

Gill Jones

The **Joseph Rowntree Foundation** has supported this project as part of its programme of research and innovative development projects, which it hopes will be of value to policy makers, practitioners and service users. The facts presented and views expressed in this report are, however, those of the author and not necessarily those of the Foundation.

Published for the Joseph Rowntree Foundation by YPS

ISBN 1 84263 076 8 (paperback)
ISBN 1 84263 081 4 (pdf: available at www.jrf.org.uk)

Prepared and printed by:
York Publishing Services Ltd
64 Hallfield Road
Layerthorpe
York YO31 7ZQ
Tel: 01904 430033; Fax: 01904 430868; E-mail: orders@yps-publishing.co.uk

Acknowledgements

A great deal of effort and expertise has been put into this publication, not by its author but by the many researchers who have been involved in this first phase of the JRF programme of research on young people. It was enlightening to read their reports and to attend many of the project advisory group's meetings. In this attempt to synthesise the findings of the programme, a degree of selectivity has been inevitable. It is certain, therefore, that I have not been able to give due and equal weight to all the points they have made. It is in the nature of a report like this that ideas cannot always be attributed to the individual or group that originally produced them, and I hope that this will not offend.

The report owes a great deal to many of the staff at the JRF, particularly to Pat Kneen, the original overseer of the programme, and to Marguerite Owen. It has been educational and enjoyable to participate in the Young People and Families Committee meetings chaired by Dame Margaret Booth. I am grateful to Keele University and the University of Cambridge for allowing me the time to undertake the role of Programme Adviser over the last five years. And last but not least, I would like to thank Charlie Lloyd, Principal Research Manager at the JRF, for being a good colleague and friend.

Preface

The Joseph Rowntree Foundation (JRF) programme of research on young people came about in response to the need to take a more integrative response to the problems of young people in Britain. The Young People Programme started in 1997, with the formation of the Young People and Families Committee, chaired by Dame Margaret Booth. Shortly after, the Economic and Social Research Council's Youth, Citizenship and Social Change research programme got under way, as did a programme on youth citizenship and participation funded by the Carnegie (UK) Trust. In all, it has been a productive few years for youth research. The first phase of the JRF programme (the Young People in Transition initiative) has now nearly drawn to a close, and a second phase has begun. This includes further research on transitions, a new emphasis on minority ethnic groups and evaluations of interventions.

The research programme

The first phase of the JRF programme of research on young people (aged 16–25 years) was organised around the following themes:

- Young People in Transition
- Patterns of Vulnerability and Exclusion
- Young People's Perceptions of the World
- Multiple Disadvantage.

Most of the funded projects mainly addressed the first two of these themes. The research has covered a wide geographical area, with some quantitative research covering the whole of the UK, and smaller qualitative studies based in local areas around England and Scotland. Around 18 projects comprised the first phase of the Young People Programme, of which one is still running and due to report in 2002. This report is based on the completed projects, plus other published research on young people funded by the Joseph Rowntree Foundation but undertaken within the Action in Rural Areas programme (Shucksmith, 2000) and the Work and Opportunity programme (Meadows, 2001). The projects are listed in the Appendix.

This report should be of interest to anyone who works with or for young people, as it addresses many general concerns for policy and practice. At a time when the major policy thrust is to combat social exclusion, the report shows how difficult this will be. The overwhelming finding from the studies cited is that, far from being a homogeneous group ('youth'), young people are becoming more and more sharply divided, between those who have and those who have not. Despite investment in education and training, inequality continues and even gets worse. We see polarisation of experience in every aspect of transition to adulthood – a 'Youth Divide'.

List of abbreviations

BCS70	Birth Cohort Study 1970
BHPS	British Household Panel Study
DfEE	Department for Education and Employment
DoH	Department of Health
DSS	Department of Social Security
E&W	England and Wales
EMA	Education Maintenance Allowance
ESRC	Economic and Social Research Council
ET	Education and Training
EU	European Union
FE	Further Education
FEFC	Further Education Funding Council
GNVQ	General National Vocational Qualification
HB	Housing Benefit
HE	Higher Education
HEFC	Higher Education Funding Councils

JCP	Job Creation Programme
JRF	Joseph Rowntree Foundation
JSA	Job Seekers' Allowance
LA	Local Authority
LCD	Lord Chancellor's Department
LEA	Local Education Authority
NCDS	National Child Development Study
NEET	Not in education, training or employment
NHS	National Health Service
NMW	National Minimum Wage
SEU	Social Exclusion Unit
SOVA	Society of Voluntary Associations
UK	United Kingdom
UN	United Nations
YCS	Youth Cohort Study
YT(S)	Youth Training (Scheme)

1 Youth and social exclusion

Social exclusion is a shorthand label for what can happen when individuals or areas suffer from a combination of linked problems such as unemployment, poor skills, low incomes, poor housing, high crime environments, bad health and family breakdown.
(Social Exclusion Unit, 1998a)

When New Labour came to power in 1997 with a massive programme aimed at seeking out the causes and processes of 'social exclusion', young people were targeted for a raft of policy initiatives. The policy document *Opportunity for All* (DSS, 1999) described the government's concern about what was seen as a 'cycle of disadvantage', whereby social and economic disadvantage was passed on in families from one generation to the next. A range of interventions was thus devised to interrupt this process, including policies targeted at child poverty and the promotion of marriage and family life.[1] The difficulty is that, while families are usually seen as the building bricks of a cohesive society, this can have a negative connotation – they act as a mechanism for transmitting both wealth and poverty from one generation to the next. Thus, while one thrust of government policy was to support families, some interventions aimed to disrupt more negative family processes. The extension of educational opportunity, and above all a massive welfare to work programme, is aimed at preventing the educational and economic disadvantages of one generation of a family being carried into the next generation.

This report brings together the findings of a programme of research on young people in the UK.

It explores current inequalities in youth, and considers the ways in which these have changed. It examines the causes of inequalities in youth, and proposes ways of overcoming the processes of social exclusion. First, though, it is important to understand the concept of 'youth'.

Extension of youth

'Youth' is a social construction, and the way it is understood as a concept varies across cultures and over time. Since youth first emerged as a 'stage in life' in its modern form it has been continually extended, largely as a result of government policies. Where a few decades ago it may have been possible to think about a single ordered sequence of transitions from childhood to adulthood,[2] the extension of education and training in particular has driven a wedge between the two, highlighting and extending the process of youth, but also making it far more complex (Jones, 1997).

As a working definition let us think of childhood as a period of economic dependence (on parents or other carers) and adulthood as the achievement of economic independence, though these are simplifications (as this report will show). Youth is thus somewhere between the two (Table 1), a period of semi-dependence during which transition to adult independence occurs (Jones and Wallace, 1992). This period of youth has become extended, and the transitions to adulthood have become more complex. The experience of young people growing up nowadays is likely to be very different from the kind of youth experienced by their parents.

Table 1 Extended transitions to adulthood

Childhood	Youth	Adulthood
School	College or training scheme	Labour market
Parental home	Intermediate household, living with peers or alone	Independent home
Child in family	Intermediate statuses, inc. single parenthood, cohabiting partner	Partner–parent
More secure housing	Transitional housing in youth housing market (e.g. furnished flats and bedsits)	More secure housing
'Pocket money' income	'Component' or partial income (e.g. transitional NMW)	Full adult income
Economic 'dependence'	Economic semi-dependence	Economic 'independence'

Key changes in the transition to adulthood

- The transition to adulthood can be broken down into different but *interconnected strands* or pathways (Table 1). Young people can become adult according to one criterion but not another. Thus they can become economically independent but still live in the parental home, or live independently but still with parental support.

- There is therefore *no longer a normative ordering* along a single pathway (comprising a school-to-work transition followed some years later by a household-and-family-formation transition). This kind of pathway was perhaps uniquely prevalent in the 1950s and early 1960s.

- 'Progress' to adult independence may involve *backtracking* (including drop-out from education or training, returns to the parental home, and tentative partnership formation and cohabitation).

- There are now more likely to be *intermediate stages* between leaving school and entry into the labour market, between living in the parental home and having a home of one's own, and (perhaps) between being a child in a family and being a parent or partner in one. Each of these stages is, however, potentially problematic.

- The *significance of individual events* (rites of passage perhaps) within these transitions has changed. Since household formation has become more separated from family formation transitions, leaving home has become a more important life event in itself. Similarly, leaving school becomes less significant when it is not accompanied by starting employment.

- The end product, *adult citizenship, is less secure* and less clearly defined: access to the labour market, an independent home and a stable family life is more in doubt than before. Though young people still aspire to conventional constructions of adulthood, we should beware of seeming to judge them on outdated criteria of 'success' and 'failure'.

- Perhaps one of the main changes in recent decades has been that *young people are seeking more independence.* This dynamic is likely to continue despite the lack of supporting structures, with or without state support, and with or without family support. Thus, many young people leave home without resources and despite the risk of homelessness, because they need to become independent of their parents.

- At the same time, however, the period of dependent youth has been extended. The extension of the period of dependent youth raises the question of *whom they should be dependent on.* Responsibility is being transferred from the state onto parents precisely at a time when there is increased likelihood of marital breakdown, and an increased chance that young people will not be living with their two natural parents.

- A *holistic approach* is needed to understand youth transitions. Social trends and policy interventions that affect one area of young people's lives are likely to affect other areas as well.

The ways in which this transition happens vary between social groups. Typically and historically, middle-class transitions have been more protracted than working-class ones, and middle-class families have provided economic support for longer. Women have similarly entered partnerships and become parents earlier than men (Jones, 1988). Social class and gender differences such as these may be changing, but they are not disappearing, as the report will show.

Social exclusion in youth

How do these changes in transitions to adulthood affect social exclusion and inclusion?

The relationship between the child and the wider society (citizenship) is to a great extent, and for better or worse, mediated by parents or other carers (thus, for example, welfare benefits are paid to parents rather than to children, and child poverty is measured at the level of a child's household rather than that of the individual child). Young people are possibly in an even more anomalous social position, half citizen in their own right and half citizen-by-proxy, via their parents or carers. Thus, inequalities (and advantage or disadvantage, integration and exclusion) accrue to young people in part directly as individuals, and in part indirectly via their parents. Individual characteristics may not therefore provide adequate indicators of social disadvantage and exclusion in youth: family characteristics may also need to be taken into account.

Social exclusion is generally identified where individuals are excluded from employment, housing, health care, etc. However, all young people are to some extent excluded from aspects of the wider (adult) society. They are marginalised as an age group. But young people are also a heterogeneous group, and people who are of the same age may be at different stages in their transitions to adulthood, and suffer social exclusion in different forms and to different degrees. Being 'in transition', some may not yet be seeking employment and housing, or they may not yet be taking responsibility for their own health care; others, however, may have sought these but failed to gain access to them. This creates a further set of problems for researchers seeking indicators of social exclusion.

Part of any programme of research on social exclusion in youth will concern itself with currently excluded groups: these will be the most visible, and probably also those who are identified as social problems (often meaning the problems for society, rather than the problems of society for young people). Young people who are identified as excluded and in need of support are only the tip of the iceberg, but it is they who are targeted for positive or negative intervention. These may include homeless and jobless young people and teenage parents; they may include young people who have turned to drugs, alcohol or crime. Because many dimensions of inequality may be cross-cutting, we find that many in these groups are disadvantaged by social class, gender, ethnicity and disability. In targeting the most easily identified groups, we should be careful not to close our minds to those who may be excluded or at the margins of society (perhaps even for the same reasons) but are less visible and pose fewer problems for society. Research on young people might indicate new forms and causes of social exclusion and identify hitherto unknown vulnerable groups.

Questions addressed in the research programme include

- What is 'structural disadvantage'?

- How important is social background?

- How are success and failure defined?

- Can an individual 'succeed' against the odds?

- Has choice increased?

- What is citizenship in youth?

Structure of the report

This report cannot hope to do justice to all the findings of the programme, but, by synthesising some of the main findings of individual projects (some of which are based on local communities and small samples), clear messages come across. These have implications for policy and practice. The reader is urged, however, also to read the original published reports of each project (see Bibliography and Appendix).

The overarching theme of the report is inequality in youth and this broadens out the debate from a narrower focus on social exclusion. The studies show that, far from being a homogeneous grouping, there is increasing polarisation among young people between those who experience extended transitions and those who make 'accelerated transitions', between the rich and the poor, between those with qualifications and those without. These polarisations show up in many aspects of young people's transitions, and they reflect continuing outcomes of structural inequality rather than personal agency and choice. Chapter 2 describes the new transitions through education and into the labour market, and identifies continuing inequalities of social class, gender, ethnicity and (dis)ability. Work is redefined as a continuum of experience from formal jobs to informal, even criminal, activity. Chapter 3 shows how polarisation of experience occurs in transitions leading to family and household formation, the transitions being extended for most but still 'fast track' for a minority. The continuing phenomenon of teenage pregnancy, and the societal reaction it causes, is discussed against a backcloth of extended transitions involving later partnerships and deferred parenthood.

One theme that runs through the report is the importance of the social relationships linking young people with their social contexts, and in Chapters 2 and 3 the significance of peer groups and local communities is briefly discussed. Chapter 4 considers the continuing, and potentially increasing, significance of the family of origin as a resource. The chapter starts by exploring the extent to which education can override earlier disadvantage in the form of family poverty, and shows the difficulty in attempting to change the patterns of generational transmission of advantage and disadvantage. It then describes the systems of family obligations and family relationships that can lead to the transmission of economic and cultural capital. Chapter 5 compares young people's definitions of independence with those implicit in government policies, and then considers the notion of empowerment, and particularly whether political participation can be extended among young people who remain economically dependent. The final chapter draws from the projects some implications for policy and practice.

2 Education and labour markets

The best defence against social exclusion is having a job, and the best way to get a job is to have a good education, with the right training and experience.
(Social Exclusion Unit, 1999a, p. 6)

Education will be our number one priority, and we will increase the share of national income spent on education as we decrease it on the bills of economic and social failure.
(Labour Party Manifesto 1997, quoted in Labour Party, 2001, p. 44)

In the eyes of many policy makers and politicians, education is the main solution to the problems of social exclusion. As investment in education increases, so investment in welfare provisions can decrease. This policy depends, however, on education 'working' for young people growing up. In order for it to work, access to post-16 education has to be open to all. Beyond this, however, young people and their families have to be persuaded that their personal investment is worth it, and this means that the benefits of education need to be clearly visible.

Policy context

The structures for the extension and expansion of post-16 education and training are complex. Government policies are tackling the skills deficit and unemployment among young people through a raft of provisions, including the introduction of Modern Apprenticeship, the Right to Time off for Study and the New Deal. Forms of encouragement to remain in post-16 education include means-tested Education Maintenance Allowances and Youth Cards for 16–18s. Concerns about young people who fall through this net and are not in employment, education or training (NEET) have led to the development of the Connexions Strategy (Connexions, 2000). Income Support has been restructured as the Job Seekers' Allowance. There is, in contrast, very little support for the 16-year-old school leaver. A National Minimum Wage has been introduced for over-18s, though with a lower transitional rate for young people aged 18–22 (Jones and Bell, 2000). It is stated government policy that all under-18s should be in education or training. The Labour Manifesto (Labour Party, 2001) pledges to extend higher education (HE) even further, through investment in primary and secondary education, with the aim of a majority of young people entering HE by 2010.

Changing paths to the labour market

Since 1976, the youth labour market has declined, school staying-on rates have increased and the proportion of young people entering HE has risen (Bynner *et al.*, 2002, forthcoming; Dolton *et al.*, 1999). By 2000, over 70 per cent of 16/17 year olds in the UK were in full-time education, compared with just under 50 per cent in 1984. In 2000, only 11 per cent were in employment, compared with 33 per cent in 1984 (National Statistics, 2000). Between the mid-1970s and the mid-1990s, the proportion of 16 year olds in England and Wales remaining in full-time education has more than doubled.

The political rhetoric is that this changing pattern reflects the expansion of opportunity and choice. Choices (whether to stay on at school or leave) at 16 years have certainly become more critical in recent years in terms of adult outcomes by 23 years (Dolton *et al.*, 1999, p. 69). Most young people now continue into academic or vocational further or higher education (Bynner *et al.*, 2002, forthcoming). It has been argued, though, that it may be the result of a lack of alternatives rather than because of a positive choice (e.g. Biggart and Furlong, 1996). For some school leavers, the local job opportunity *now*, however menial, is still more attractive than the vague promise of a better job in an uncertain future.

Though several studies in the programme suggest that the greater risk and uncertainty lies in *not* getting qualifications, it is quite clear from research undertaken (see especially McDowell, 2001, discussed below) that some young people do not realise this. It is also clear, though, that the benefits of education are not evenly spread (see Berthoud, 1999, for example). The challenge for policy makers now is to persuade 'non-traditional students' (young people who might previously have taken the work route, rather than the education route, to better jobs) to take up the education and training opportunities available. This 'choice' involves deferring both their entry into employment and their economic independence (Forsyth and Furlong, 2000), and there is therefore a lot of persuading to be done.

JRF research

Several studies funded by the JRF have explored the different patterns of transition from school to work, and some have found that new divisions are appearing among young people entering adulthood. There are winners and losers in the system. For example, the longer-term labour market destinations of stayers-on in education are more and more distinguished from those of early school leavers, and a polarisation is occurring between the majority who are benefiting and the minority who are not. This division is not simply the result of a distinction between those with ability and those without.

In this chapter, these divisions are explored. First of all, the basic and dramatically changing map of transition to the labour market is described. We examine the outcomes at the opposite ends of the polarisation, university graduates and early school leavers. This is where the evidence of the value of education lies. Then the chapter considers factors leading to 'success' and 'failure' according to the policy makers' model. First, the myth that all with the ability can gain access to higher education is exploded. We do not live in a meritocracy: some with the ability are not able to continue into higher education (HE), or drop out before the completion

of their studies. Then we examine 'success' and 'failure' in the labour market. Again, what we find is not a meritocracy, but a system that can disadvantage young people on the basis of social class, gender, ethnicity, disability and the communities in which they live.

Polarisation

The analysis of large national data sets makes it possible to see the extent to which new divisions are occurring in young people's experiences. Using data from two national birth cohort studies (of young people born 12 years apart), Bynner and his colleagues (2002, forthcoming) mapped the changes in patterns of transition to adulthood.[1] They looked for evidence that the social and policy changes (including the increased educational opportunity and participation) had achieved a measurably beneficial effect over the 12 years, by comparing the two cohorts. They found that young people became better off only to a limited extent. The study identified three areas where comparison of data from the two cohorts shows instead strong evidence of a trend towards increasing polarisation, in:

- *occupations* (between career jobs and insecure ones)

- *qualifications* (between those with higher qualifications and those with no qualifications)

- *earnings* (between the better paid and the low paid).

The employment of young people has been marginalised. Many of the jobs typically held by school leavers have disappeared, and opportunities for 16-year-old school leavers have reduced. Traditional craft apprenticeships for young men and clerical/secretarial jobs for young women have been replaced by sales occupations, often part-time and low paid. These occupational shifts in the labour market have affected recruitment patterns, and may have worsened the relative labour market position of the declining but still very significant group of young people who do not go on to further or higher education. There are now few alternatives to educational success. The 'work route' – involving apprenticeship and working experience, rather than academic qualifications – previously offered another route to upward mobility, but craft apprenticeships have all but disappeared to be replaced by training schemes, and 'stepping-stone jobs' no longer exist. This has affected those without qualifications and from low-income households in particular, as they are more likely to experience early unemployment, which in turn has a longer-term impact ('scarring' effect) both on later employment and on earning power. The researchers found that:

> Despite the longest sustained period of economic growth in the last thirty years and a massive decline in the numbers of young people available for work, a 'core' of unemployment among young people remains stubbornly present.
> (Bynner *et al.*, 2002, forthcoming, Chapter 6)

As the better qualified stay on in education and training in their youth, so the youth labour market increasingly becomes a market for less-qualified labour. A gap is thus appearing between those holding good educational qualifications and those who do not. Higher-level qualifications are growing in importance, as they reduce the risk of later unemployment and increase earnings power. The rise in educational qualifications may favour those who would have done reasonably well in the labour market anyway. This brings into question the added value of education. Bynner *et al.* (2002, forthcoming) suggest that it is unsurprising that a significant core rejects the education route, pointing out that young people are being pushed into a post-16 learning process that was originally designed to provide specialist knowledge for entry into university courses, not preparation for the labour

market. They argue therefore that post-16 education needs to be made relevant to the needs of the wider range of young people now entering it.

On average, young people now are 'better off' financially than their equivalent age cohort were 15 years ago. However, income disparities have grown, both relative to adult earnings and among young people. Post-16 qualifications are the most powerful influence on earnings, and for men are becoming increasingly so. Young workers may be more qualified, but they are also less experienced, and this may also affect their earnings at first. Early unemployment continues to have a downward, 'scarring', effect on later earnings. The evidence confirms that remaining in the education system is beneficial in the longer term but suggests that, as access widens and qualifications become more common, this benefit may become eroded. Bynner *et al.* (2002, forthcoming) found that the earnings value of a degree, though still high, had been reduced in the last 15 years.[2]

This polarisation between those who stay on in education and gain qualifications, and those who leave school and risk bad jobs, low pay and unemployment is only the most visible outcome of inequality among young people. In order to comprehend why this polarisation occurs, it is important to move beyond it to understand the more complex underlying structure of opportunity and risk for young people in Britain today.

Structures of disadvantage

The main dimensions of social inequality continue to be social class, gender, ethnicity and disability, but the ways in which these structures interact to perpetuate inequality can be complex.

In statistical overviews, Dolton *et al.* (1999) and Stafford *et al.* (1999) explored the determinants of success and lack of success in the labour market. Dolton *et al.*'s study of barriers and bridges was based on outcomes at 23 years.[3] They found that social class continues to have a strong effect. Young people from disadvantaged backgrounds (large families in rented accommodation, parents in lower manual work) did less well than their middle-class peers, and there was a long-term effect of school truancy. Stafford *et al.* (1999) found a higher risk of under-achievement among unqualified and inexperienced young people and those with health problems. A significant factor was the educational level of the mother. In other words, in assessing the impact of socio-economic status on youth transitions, it is not just economic capital that counts. The level of cultural capital in the home is clearly also significant. This is reflected in parents' own experience of and attitude to education, which affects both whether parents encourage their children to achieve educationally and whether they are willing to 'put their money where their mouths are' and provide financial support for them to do so (see below and Chapter 4).

Cross-cutting social-class inequalities, there are also inequalities of gender, ethnicity and disability.

- *Gender* differences continue to be significant. One of the dramatic recent changes has been in the proportion of women staying on in education to the extent that they now outnumber young men in HE. Stafford *et al.* (1999),[4] who explored changing gender variation in education and the labour market, suggest that academic qualifications are more important for women, given the shift in the occupational structure from manual manufacturing jobs to non-manual service jobs. Educational achievements are not necessarily reflected in women's occupational status, however. Despite the 'feminisation' of the labour market, women's greater advantage in education is therefore not carried through into labour market outcomes at higher levels.

- There is variation between *ethnic groups* both in participation in post-16 education and in labour market outcomes (Berthoud, 1999). Proportions of white and Caribbean men

achieving A levels have been falling behind those of other ethnic populations. Berthoud found that, though men in some minority ethnic groups stayed longer in education than white men, this was sometimes because they took longer to obtain the same qualifications. They also had higher rates of unemployment than those who had obtained equivalent qualifications more quickly. Educational success among African groups was thus not matched by labour market success, and a black African graduate was seven times more likely to be unemployed than a white graduate. The analysis revealed stratification between three broad ethnic groupings: 'whites' and Indians, with a fairly consistent and relatively low risk of unemployment; Pakistanis and Bangladeshis, with a consistently high risk of unemployment; and Caribbeans and Africans, with a high average risk of unemployment but wide variation within the group. Berthoud found that inequalities between ethnic groups were increasing. This suggests, first, that the education system is itself biased against ethnic minorities and, second, that education is failing to overcome race discrimination (Berthoud, 1999).

- Two studies specifically revealed the disadvantage experienced by many young people with *disabilities*. One sample comprised an educated minority and 'the rest', a less educated majority (Hendey and Pascall, 2002). A study of black young people with disabilities found that many had negative experiences of the education system and felt this was because professionals' expectations of them were low because of their race, culture and/or disability (Bignall and Butt, 2000).[5]

Many of the barriers to success are thus beyond individual control. The findings should be of interest to those who believe that disadvantaged young people can succeed 'against the odds', or even that multiply disadvantaged young people necessarily fail. They also indicate that success in one sphere (education) is not necessarily matched with success in another sphere (the labour market), and that the concept of 'success' is sometimes treated in too simplistic a way.

Perceptions of higher education

Against this background of widening participation but continuing inequalities, a Scottish study (Forsyth and Furlong, 2000) explored the reasons for the persisting under-representation in HE of those from lower socio-economic backgrounds.[6] The mechanisms of persisting inequality in access to HE must be understood if the stated policy of ever-increasing participation is to be achieved. The vast majority of disadvantaged young people still enter the labour market on leaving school. This is mainly because they are less likely to achieve the entry requirements (suggesting that schools are still letting them down),[7] but even those meeting HE entry requirements are still less likely to attempt to enter HE than those from middle-class backgrounds with the same qualifications. This raises questions about the criteria used by young people and their parents in deciding whether or not to stay in education. These decisions are clearly not made on the basis of academic achievement alone.

The study therefore looked for the barriers that may operate to prevent academically able young people from attending HE. Some young people felt neglected by the school system, and blamed under-achieving schools, where teachers focused on the less motivated pupils ('it was the idiots that got all the attention') to the detriment of the rest (Forsyth and Furlong, 2000, p. 35). For others, there were financial disincentives from applying to universities. In summary:

- Schools failed to provide enough information. Very few young people realised when they were still at school that they might be exempt from paying tuition fees – and this might have been a deterrent to disadvantaged school students.

- Nearly all the parents in the study approved of their son or daughter entering HE, and most were willing to provide a high level of financial support, but some were unable to do so.

- Some young people were deterred from HE altogether by the prospect of debts.

For those who did go to university, financial considerations affected their work and their ability to take part in 'student life'. They had to weigh up part-time work (which helped fend off debt, but encroached on study and social time) with student loans (which resulted in debt). The biggest source of income for students was from loans (68 per cent), though some students found them difficult to arrange. Loans were supplemented for many students (55 per cent) by earnings from part-time work, even at an early stage in their student careers. Part-time work in term and full-time in the vacations was essential for many students, but associated travel costs eroded both their incomes and their study time, and impacted on their academic performance.[8] The resulting tensions could lead to drop-out:

Trying to balance work and the university, now that is the hardest thing, because for a while there I had a five-day-a-week job and it was running straight from uni to work and concentrating more on work than uni. So it's really trying to balance work and uni that is about the hardest thing.
(Quoted in Forsyth and Furlong, 2000, p. 39)

Things were a lot different in my head than what they were going to be when I went there. I did like being at university. I liked the people and that. I enjoyed the course. I thought it was really good, but at the end of the day it just got back to money again. That was the thing that was going to stop me.
(Quoted in Forsyth and Furlong, 2000, p. 46)

I didn't feel working class until I went to uni.
(Quoted in Forsyth and Furlong, 2000, pp. 36–7)

The study shows how student life is changing, as the concept of the campus as an intellectual community gives way to the campus as commuter-land, with students commuting to their courses from home or to their jobs from campus. For disadvantaged young people in particular, there is no division between education and employment, which are pursued hand in hand. If HE is to be made more attractive, there would need to be grants (or an extension of bursaries), provision of low-cost, good-standard student accommodation and subsidised travel.[9] It is still a long way from being an egalitarian system.

Perceptions of the youth labour market

Working-class men
Stafford *et al.* (1999, p. 3) refer to 'the feminisation of society'. For those who do not sign up to education, who reject the school ethos with its 'swots' and 'ear'oles' (Willis, 1977), there are fewer and fewer jobs. It has been argued that the kind of traditional masculinity that valorises manual labour is now under threat, and that those young working-class men who persist with this view of masculinity are reduced to affirming their male identities through aggression and intolerance (especially of women, gays and ethnic minorities) (Mac an Ghaill, 1996). They represent a minority. In general, male gender identities are in the process of transformation – there are now many different ways in which men can be men.

A study by Linda McDowell (2001) focused on white working-class young men without qualifications and found them unaware of many of the changes going on around them. McDowell stresses that it is not *all* men who are now disadvantaged in education and in the labour market, but some – particularly those who are working class and living in poor neighbourhoods. Her study of low-achieving school leavers in Sheffield and Cambridge shows how they understood their gender identities, and interpreted success and failure. Though the young men in both towns distinguished between anti-school 'nutters'/'hards' and pro-school 'boffs'/'boffins', most did not place themselves within this distinction, referring to themselves as normal or average. Nevertheless, theirs was an assertive masculinity and they were disparaging about girls, seeing boys as superior (the ways in which this impacted on their attitudes to young women are discussed in the next chapter). They denied a crisis of masculinity, believing that boys and girls achieved equally at school if not in the labour market. In practice, several had started work in the service sector, holding down jobs which were available to both men and women.

They had little awareness of the realities of the labour market. They had a clear sense of the kinds of job that they considered appropriate for men, and expressed no fears about finding one. McDowell comments that they:

... had relatively little sense of the extent to which economic restructuring had transformed opportunities for men and women. It was perhaps surprising how little they were aware of the changed economic circumstances that awaited them and they had no sense at all that they might not be able to achieve and maintain the traditional pattern of working class life in which they were the main breadwinner.
(McDowell, 2001, p. 21)

McDowell came both to respect and to admire their tenacity, but also to regret their limited horizons, concluding that most of them had far more personal and social skills than their examination performances would suggest. In her view, they did not conform to commonly held views about low-ability working-class young men (McDowell, 2001, p. 35). These young men emphasised jobs over education, despite their jobs often being temporary or casual or less than full-time. The study thus raises the question of how they could be won over to the educational ethos, given their lack of awareness of its increased importance.

Alternative careers

One study based in Teesside (Johnston *et al.*, 2000a) set out to explore how young people move into adulthood when they live in a place that displays all the objective measures of social exclusion in extreme form. The study area has been in rapid decline, suffering high levels of structural unemployment. In 1998, only 6 per cent of school leavers found jobs, and around 15 per cent were not in education, training or employment. One of the aims of the research was to understand the extent to which young people's life chances were determined by their backgrounds, or whether they might be helped to overcome early disadvantage. This is the 'against the odds' question: to what extent can young people achieve when the odds appear to be stacked against them? The study found that some do. Despite growing up in the same neighbourhood, young people's experiences differed widely. Early family experiences, including bereavement and homelessness, could be very significant. The researchers found that processes of social exclusion could be identified at an early stage of the life course. Thus, truancy and school exclusion were associated with later involvement with drug use, delinquency and crime. Early interventions were therefore important, and indeed key moments and experiences, and particular

people and policies, were found to have a very significant intervening effect (Johnston *et al.*, 2000a, p. 24; see also Britton *et al.*, 2002, forthcoming).

The research explored 'alternative careers', recognising the possibility of overlap between:

- 'traditional careers' of regular employment in the economic mainstream

- careers involving little engagement with employment or education and repeated or continuous spells of unemployment

- careers involving extensive or repeated engagement with more informal economic activity (such as volunteering, self-employment and cash-in-hand 'fiddly work')

- education and training careers that delay entry into the labour market

- domestic or home-centred careers (mainly child care and domestic labour)

- criminal careers (withdrawal from ET and employment in favour of repeated and long-term offending).

Though most of the sample valued and aspired to a 'proper job', only a minority had been able to secure long-term or rewarding employment. 'Proper jobs' in the local youth labour market tended to be badly paid ('shit jobs'). Nevertheless, no one in the sample 'could identify any positive aspects to worklessness and the majority were prepared to work for low pay in poor conditions' (Johnston *et al.*, 2000a, p. 27). In practice, many without proper jobs did occasional work, sometimes merged with criminal activity.

Criminal careers

While official understandings of remunerative 'work' are restricted to activity in the formal labour market, there is not necessarily any such distinction in young people's minds.[10] Some young people in the North East even spoke of their offending activity as work, it being the 'family business'.

I would regard it as work 'cause it was a routine thing ... Getting up in the morning, getting ready, going out, going to work, coming home. Our mam'd have the tea there ready for us. We'd give her 60 quids ... It's just like going to work.
(Quoted in Johnston *et al.*, 2000a, p. 29)

According to Johnston *et al.* (2000a), those involved in 'criminal careers' were a more homogeneous group than those on other career pathways, consisting, typically, of young people who had begun to disengage from school at 12 or 13, had from an early age participated with their peers in street drinking, drug use and petty crime, and had later progressed to more serious crime and drug use. An influx of heroin in the mid-1990s transformed the local criminal economy and had a devastating impact on the local community, including creation of a link between drugs and crime (a local economy of crime far less associated with drug use had existed previously). Out of a total of 98 young people, 65 said they had used drugs, including 21 who said they had used heroin.

Both Canter (unpublished) and Johnston *et al.* (2000a, p. 29) found a close association between drug use and offending, and both studies examined reasons why early criminal careers tend to peter out among most young offenders. Johnston *et al.* (2000a) found that some young people stopped offending when they became engaged in training or college courses, or in temporary, informal or legitimate (though usually casual) work:

I've settled down a lot. It's no good to nobody going to jail, stuff like that. As you get older you get sick of being a nuisance. You think to yourself, 'it's about time I settled down'. And it does settle you down, getting a girlfriend and having a kid. It doesn't half. You gotta think 'I've gotta be responsible now'. You just keep away from things and then you just, sort of like, sort yourself out.
(Matthew, aged 25, quoted in Johnston *et al.*, 2000a, p. 11)

Canter (unpublished) found that offending ended with the development of new relationships and responsibilities (e.g. settling down with a partner and child), or arrival at a crisis point when the offending behaviour became unsustainable. However, Canter also found a gender difference, with women more likely to desist because of relationships.

Young people and their communities

One of the most important sources of variation in the experiences of young people lies in their geographical distribution, affecting their access to local education and job opportunities. Those in disadvantaged neighbourhoods, whether in urban areas or rural ones, have to be able to get to more prosperous areas to study or work, or become resigned to the lower level of opportunity locally available, making compromises or lowering their aspirations where necessary. Getting out means obtaining financial support, whether from the state, an employer, or a family member. Staying in a disadvantaged area may require the protection that community solidarity can sometimes provide. There are, however, dangers in stereotyping a community as disadvantaged: within any area there are likely to be pockets of affluence, or some areas worse than others. This applies both to rural areas (Forsyth and Furlong, 2000) and to urban ones (Johnston *et al.*, 2000a).

Community solidarity
Community solidarity confirms the distinction between the community and the world outside. In the disadvantaged community in the urban North East, it allowed the area to tolerate negative labelling by outsiders (Johnston *et al.*, 2000a). The negative views of employers led to post-code discrimination in recruitment practices and affected some who were wanting job interviews. Equally, young people in the community who were wanting

to get off drugs knew that they had to make a positive effort to form different social networks outside the area. Nevertheless, informal social networks in the community helped many individuals manage their lives (whether as workers, unemployed, drug-users or criminals).

There are advantages in staying on in a deprived area, whether urban or rural. Moving from a disadvantaged area means the loss of local networks. In the North East:

> *The parochialism and localism that limited their career opportunities also brought advantages. They felt connected to the place and, if they moved to another town or city, they would become disconnected from the local networks that they had learned to rely on for socialising and support, in searching for jobs, decent training schemes and suitable accommodation, and in coping with crime.*
> (Johnston et al., 2000a, p. 23)

A similar point is made in relation to rural areas, by Pavis *et al.* (2000, p. 11), who point out that:

> *The reality was that most of these young people lacked the skills necessary to make them competitive in the type of jobs that were advertised nationally. Moreover, moving to another area (rural or urban) necessarily led to the loss of social networks, which provided much of the young people's employment. The fact that most low-skilled employment was secured through word of mouth and local reputation gave the local young people an important comparative advantage within their community.*

Mobility and migration

The emphasis of government intervention has been on poor neighbourhoods in urban areas such as the one studied by Johnston *et al.* (2000a), but spatial disadvantage is not restricted to the inner cities (Shucksmith, 2000). The lower population density in rural areas, the influx of city-dwellers seeking out their own rural idylls, the media emphasis on fox hunting or farming crises, all combine to conceal the existence of a rural poor.

Though transport is a widespread problem for young people unable to buy and maintain private transport or get subsidies to use public transport (namely, Forsyth and Furlong, 2000 on the problems of students), this is a particular problem for young people in rural areas (Pavis *et al.*, 2000; Storey and Brannen, 2000). Stafford *et al.* (1999) found that young unemployed with a driving licence were twice as likely to re-enter employment as those without, though they note that this could be a proxy measure for other factors:

> *Before you can even look for a job ... you've got to know which areas you can get to easily so that you can be reliable. Before you get a house, you've got to get a job. So you've got to have money before you start, to get a car, to get a job, or whatever.*
> (Quoted in Rugg and Jones, 1999, p. 19)

> *The job centre doesn't look favourably on you if you're looking for work, live in a village and have no car ... your chance of a job is almost zero. And no job, no money for a car.*
> (Quoted in Storey and Brannen, 2000, p. 9)

The interconnectedness of youth transitions becomes particularly visible in the countryside, where education-to-labour-market transitions interact (or conflict) with family transitions within a context of migration. The stark choice is often to stay on in a rural area, start an early family and remain dependent on a limited structure of local opportunities, or to migrate away to areas where jobs and housing are more readily available (Jones, 2001). Unemployment and homelessness may become visible in towns, but originate in the countryside.

Summary

The emphasis of current policy makers is to increase the skills and qualification levels of the UK labour force, by extending education and training opportunities and encouraging young people to improve their employment chances through education, rather than enter the labour market before they have gained the skills and qualifications they will need. There has been a massive increase in young people continuing in post-16 education and going on to university. This is not across the board. Although more and more young people are beginning to take the longer paths into the labour market previously associated with the educated middle class in Britain, there is a more identifiable disadvantaged group of working-class young people who are missing out on the extension and expansion of education and training.

The research has shown some of the ways in which social inclusion and exclusion are reproduced. One way is through generational transmission of cultural capital, which continues to be seen in the varying extent to which parents hold a belief in education and transmit this to their children, giving them encouragement and financial support to continue their studies. Another way is in the transmission of economic capital, in a world in which wealth and poverty are polarised. In Chapter 4, the significance of the cultural and economic capital of the family of origin in reproducing or overcoming disadvantage is discussed, and the scope for education to overcome this effect assessed.

Education policies depend on public belief in the value of education, 'the education ethos'. People need to be sure that their personal investment in education will be worth it in the longer term. Unfortunately, though, there is evidence that the increase in qualifications is resulting in a reduction in their value. The earnings bonus of gaining a degree is less apparent. Though more women enter HE, the beneficial extent is not carried through into the labour market. Access to HE is difficult for young people in some minority ethnic groups but, even among those who do gain a degree, there is still disadvantage in the labour market. Education does not therefore 'work' for everyone. Further, the social benefits associated with university life are reducing. The wider, but unsupported, access to higher education is putting new financial strains on families and young people themselves. Drop-out from courses is becoming more common and, for those from poor families who are sticking it out as students, life can be a complex balancing of study and work. Students graduate from universities with large debts instead of increased social capital. The benefits of education are not always apparent.

In contrast, while many young people and their parents still hold a strong work ethic, this appears to be barely supported by government. Perhaps more support for the youth labour market is now needed. As the youth labour market (for teenagers) becomes reduced to casual and low-paid work, young people may become involved in a range of formal and informal economic activity, sometimes alongside their education and training courses. They are neither willing nor able to postpone the economic independence that a job can provide. Where jobs are not available, then they may resort to the informal labour market. Work is clearly still important to young people and we must recognise its continuing significance in their lives.

3 Home and family

Alongside the complex transitions from school into the labour market are equally complex 'domestic' transitions from being a child in the parental home to setting up an independent home, perhaps with a partner and children of one's own. The extension of the period of economic dependence in youth, brought about by the extension of education, loss of labour market opportunities and changes to the welfare structure, has had an impact on young people's ability to make the transition into independent living, away from their parents.

Policy context

The policy context of domestic transitions is less easy to identify than that for school-to-work transitions. There is such a strong assumption that parents will provide support for their older children (see Jones and Bell, 2000) that it is difficult to find policies aimed at supporting young people leaving the parental home or starting family life, other than those that focus on problematic aspects of these transitions: homelessness, teenage pregnancy, etc. Despite the moral support for conventional transitions to domestic independence, there is little practical support. Thus, the housing market for young people is almost entirely in the private sector or linked to education or employment. Housing Benefit (HB) is no longer available to students; since 1996, HB has been based on the average market rent for a room in a shared local property (Single Room Rent) even if the claimant is living alone. The dwindling public rented sector is still targeted at social housing for families. It is therefore still hard for a young single person to leave home, and there are more of them needing to do so.

On the other hand, support for young people experiencing problems is conditional on 'good behaviour' (Jones and Bell, 2000). Foyer accommodation for homeless young people is dependent on their agreeing to work. A New Deal for Lone Parents is intended to encourage young mothers to take up employment rather than stay on benefits. These initiatives may enable young people to escape the poverty trap but they also have moral overtones. As Lewis (1998, p. 274) has pointed out with regard to lone mothers, those who do not conform to convention are labelled as irresponsible scroungers – the modern equivalent of the 'undeserving poor'.

Changing household and family formation

The main shift in patterns of family formation reflects a changing relationship between its constituent parts: marriage, sex and childbirth. Sexual activity among young people is increasingly seen as an end in itself, rather than as a part of a loving relationship or a means of having children (though the Social Exclusion Unit [1999a] report on *Teenage Pregnancy* reported gender differences in this respect, with men highlighting 'opportunity' and women 'love' as the basis of sexual experience). For those in partnerships, childbirth has been deferred, and family building is seen as part of a life plan which has to take into account the requirements of a career, as well as the economic demands of home-ownership and a social life.

In many respects, there has been an extension of the period of dependent youth, with young adults drawing on the resources of their families of origin for longer, with higher ages at marriage and the birth of the first child. More young people are now following the type of transition previously associated with the middle class. But not all young people can do this successfully and, in the patterns of 'domestic' transitions made by young people today, there is further polarisation of opportunity and choice. Evidence of this polarisation lies in the high numbers of teenagers who become parents (Bynner *et al.*, 2002, forthcoming; Social Exclusion Unit, 1999a), and who leave the parental home facing the risk of homelessness (Jones, 1995).

JRF research

This chapter summarises the findings of several projects on three strands of the transition to adult independence: leaving home and household formation; partnership formation; and parenthood. Conventionally, these formed a unitary and one-way transition, more extended among the middle class than among the working class. While the working-class pattern a generation or so ago was for the three strands to be closely combined, in practice many young people now leave home as single people and may have children before they form marital partnerships, or may live in childless partnerships for some time before having children. More people of working-class origin are – with greater affluence – following middle-class patterns of extended transitions, leaving behind a residual group that continues to follow traditional practices, in the face of societal reconstruction of these practices into social problems. It is a group best characterised by poverty.

In each strand of transition, the research found both extended and accelerated pathways, in a polarisation based largely on social class. These patterns are now explored and the problems identified with both fast- and slow-track transitions highlighted.

Leaving home

Young people have a very strong sense of a growing need to be independent from their parents, and leaving home is clearly associated with greater autonomy and freedom to act as one chooses.[1] Because of this, the leaving-home transition has become dissociated from marriage and family formation, and has become a significant aspect of the transition to adulthood. Like other strands in the transition to adulthood, there has been a polarisation of experience, between those who stay longer in the parental home and those who leave early (often because they have to).

Establishing an independent home

Only a few decades ago, marriage provided the means by which many young people left the parental home. Changing patterns of leaving home, including leaving home as a single young person to study or to work, rather than to live with a partner, mean that the housing demand from young people has significantly changed and increased. The demand now being made on the housing market is not matched by housing supply, which continues to be geared to families. In order to be able to afford the available housing, young people have to find their own solutions, one of which is to share with friends, an increasingly common alternative to early marriage. Increasingly, those who can afford it are also living alone. There may be some advantages in the 'single lifestyle' (see Heath and Kenyon, 2001; Jones and Martin, 1999); there are also disadvantages (according to Bynner *et al.*, 2002, forthcoming).

Living in the parental home

It has become more common for young people to use the parental home as a continuing resource, returning to stay there if necessary (Jones, 1995). Some young people, however, are staying on longer in the parental home, because of the cost of leaving or the lack of appropriate housing. Bynner *et al.* (2002, forthcoming) found that around one-third of men and one-fifth of women were living in the parental home at age 26, and that these proportions had not increased over the previous 12 years, although they may have included increasing numbers who had left home and later returned.

Living in the parental home can be beneficial, if the parents are in employment. Unemployed young men living in the parental home or with kin were more likely to move into employment than those who did not (including living alone and living in a couple). Stafford *et al.* (1999) suggest that this is because living in the parental home helps a young person obtain secure employment (through financial support, encouragement, job information and other resources).[2] One explanation is offered by Lloyd (1999), who found that young men in low-paid work and living away from the parental home could get caught in a poverty trap which prevented them from raising their horizons and seeking career jobs, while, for those living in the parental home, family support allowed more space to plan a career.

Housing problems

The parental home is not a resource for everyone, as studies of homelessness have shown.[3] Many young people experience housing problems, because of the lack of affordable and appropriate housing for single young people. In cases where a young person has no choice but to leave home, whether to take up a job, look for work, study, or because of family conflict, the risk of homelessness is high, though reducing with age (Jones, 1995). It cannot be assumed that parents will allow their adult children to remain in the parental home, and indeed there is no legal obligation for them to do so (Jones and Bell, 2000). Much therefore depends on the underlying quality of a young person's relationship with their parents or carers, at a time when it may be under a lot of stress. Mediation services may provide a solution for some homeless young people, for example, but, as Smith *et al.* (1998) point out, others would be better helped to build an independent life for themselves.

Living in the parental home can disguise young people's personal poverty (Pavis *et al.*, 2000). Young people in rural areas have to live longer in the parental home because there is no alternative other than buying, and may thus constitute 'hidden homeless'. Students in Scotland tend to enrol at local universities, mainly for financial reasons, since it may allow them to remain in the parental home, but their choice of a local university might involve compromise (Forsyth and Furlong, 2000). Leaving home in rural areas is affected by the local labour and housing markets: leaving home is either

later, in order to marry/cohabit locally, or earlier, involving migration away to study or work (Jones, 2001). It is also affected by family relationships, and those without supportive families are likely to migrate to a nearby town or city, losing also other support and employment networks (Rugg and Jones, 1999, p. 33).

Hendey and Pascall (2002) studied the transitions to adulthood of young people with disabilities,[4] for whom independent living has a particular significance. Disabled young people were less likely than young people in general to be living independently of their parents or to be in paid work. Leaving home can be very difficult emotionally as well as practically and financially.

Partnerships

As divorce rates have increased, marriage rates have gone down over the last few decades, and more and more people cohabit before, or instead of, marrying (Bynner *et al.*, 2002, forthcoming). Median ages of first marriage in 1990 were 24.9 for women and 26.8 for men, compared with 21.4 for women and 23.4 for men in 1970, an increase of about three-and-a-half years. Prior to marriage, cohabiting partnerships have become the norm (Utting, 1995).

Despite the increasing instability of marriage as a social institution (Bynner *et al.*, 2002, forthcoming), most young people still aspire to conventional family ideals. A study of disadvantaged young people in Teesside, for example, found that despite (or because of?) their own upbringing and family experiences, the young people interviewed saw their futures conventionally as 'nice husband or wife, nice house and nice car' (Johnston *et al.*, 2000a, p. 26). Similarly, the main ambition for the young men interviewed by McDowell was to 'settle down in a good job, buy a car and get married', usually in that order (McDowell, 2001, p. 21). Hendey and Pascall (2002) found that young people with disabilities shared these conventional aspirations despite the barriers in the way of achieving them. And, although one homeless young woman in Gillies *et al.*'s (2001) study of young people and their families said: '[family] doesn't mean anything to me any more, 'cos as far as I am concerned, I ain't got no family' (p. 28), nevertheless – like so many others – her ambition was to build a family that corresponded to the conventional ideal.

Slow and fast lanes

Despite this consensus about the domestic ideal, there are significant differences in the ways young people make domestic transitions. Working-class and female transitions tend to be more condensed and earlier, while middle-class and male transitions tend to be more protracted and later (Jones, 1988). This polarisation is increasing. Bynner *et al.* (2002, forthcoming) identify a 'widening gap between those on the fast and the slow lanes to adulthood'. For those in the slow lane, the pathway to family formation is deferred or prolonged, thus, young men in particular who were single at 19 were more likely still to be single at 26. The fast lane involved early partnership formation and parenthood, followed by partnership breakdown and lone parenthood. They also find an association with school-to-labour-market transitions: accelerated transitions being commonest among the least educated, and prolonged transitions among the most advantaged.

> Teenage motherhood ... epitomises the problem: early school leaving, no qualifications, poor job or youth training, pregnancy and childbirth, poor prospects of ever getting a decent job, family poverty.
> (Bynner *et al.*, 2000, quoted in Bynner *et al.*, 2002, forthcoming)

This is a continuation and reformulation of the long-established social-class patterns, in the context of increased working-class affluence. The new disadvantaged are defined instead by poverty. The finding does not override the continuing gender difference in paths to adulthood, whereby women enter partnerships and parenthood at a younger age than men. The implications of the findings suggest, though, that fast-track and slow-track transitions could be equally problematic. While early partnership and parenthood may be associated with a high rate of marital breakdown and lone parenthood, the slow-track transition may result in more people remaining single and childless.

Parenthood

> Teenage pregnancy is often a cause and a consequence of social exclusion.
> (Social Exclusion Unit, 1999a, p. 17)

Teenage pregnancy has been identified as a significant problem in the UK, and is now targeted for government intervention (Social Exclusion Unit, 1999a). The UK teenage conception rate among 15–19 year olds was around 65 per thousand in 1998 (one of the highest rates in Europe), but has decreased since the late 1960s and early 1970s, when it was 80 per thousand. Teenage pregnancy is associated with lower socio-economic background and with greater health risk to the child (National Statistics, 2000). It is unclear therefore whether the latter problem lies with the age of the mother or her socio-economic circumstances.

As Bynner *et al.* (2002, forthcoming) point out, it is ironic that teenage parenthood, once a common occurrence for women, has now been constructed as a social problem, and manifestation (and cause) of social exclusion. They argue that:

> While this pressure ... to postpone parenthood for the sake of qualifications and employment experience makes obvious sense in today's labour market, the price to be paid may be increasing numbers who never become parents.

The decline in the birth rate, when considered alongside the ageing of society, the increase in the proportion of the population which is 'dependent' and the prohibitive cost of state welfare, suggests that it is childlessness rather than teenage parenthood which will cause the greatest problems in the future. In general, the age at which people have children in the UK has increased, in association with the trend towards a higher age at first marriage. Thus, the mean age among women in England and Wales at first birth was 26.5 in 1994, compared with 23.9 in 1964, and during the same period childlessness doubled to 20 per cent by the age of 35 years. These figures are significant in showing how young people's current transitions are different from those of their parents' generation. Commentators point out, though, that the 1960s was a very untypical era, and that in some respects current patterns are closer to those of the 1930s (MacRae, 1999).

Teenage pregnancy

There is no evidence that young people in the UK start sexual activity at a younger age than their peers elsewhere in Europe. One of the main reasons for teenage pregnancy is the low level of contraceptive use among young people (Allen and Bourke Dowling, 1999). Bynner et al. (2002, forthcoming) found teenage parenthood to be associated with relative family poverty (free school meals, rented accommodation and overcrowding) among the 1958 cohort, but not the later cohort, for whom qualifications were more significant. However, for both cohorts, teenage pregnancy was associated with having a young mother oneself.[5] Early motherhood thus follows an intergenerational pattern. As Bynner and his colleagues indicate (2002, forthcoming):

> This consistent and striking evidence in young women's life courses of intergenerational transfer poses perhaps one of the most serious challenges for the government's social exclusion agenda.

The government has pledged to halve the teenage pregnancy rate within ten years. The policy thrust is not only to prevent teenage conceptions, but also to offer support to young mothers to allow them to participate in the labour market. The greatest need is probably for subsidised child care, but in some areas formal child-care provision is very limited and many young mothers have to rely on their relatives. Not all can do so. Young women in rural Scotland had to prioritise their family responsibilities over any career ambitions (Pavis et al., 2000). For lone parents living in rural areas it is therefore hard to escape from the poverty trap:

> I'm stuck here now really until he's a lot older and until I can find somewhere else to live, somewhere cheaper, or until some poor bloke comes along and marries me.
> (Rugg and Jones, 1999, p. 25)

Abortion

Across the UK, 43 per cent of conceptions in unmarried women aged under 18 in 1998 led to an abortion, but the abortion rate varies considerably. Tabberer et al. (2000) investigated the process of decision making which might lead to abortions among teenage women.[6] For most, pregnancy had been a shock, and the decision whether or not to continue with it was a difficult one. Unlike pregnancy, which was widely discussed, abortion was not. Most of those opting for abortion had kept it from their parents. Family support may, however, be particularly important in the face of local pressures and prevalent anti-abortion views. The abortion might be viewed with considerable ambivalence by the young woman herself, but the fear of being 'stuck with a child' can be influential:

> I did want to keep it, but I don't know. I think, looking back, I still don't think what I did was right, 'cos I don't agree with abortion, but I knew that, in the long term, it would be the right thing that I did – 'cos now I'd be stuck at home with a kid, with a 3-year-old kid.
> (Quoted in Tabberer et al., 2000, p. 36)

The research pointed to a need for abortion counselling during early pregnancy, and for information about abortion to be included in sex education in schools. Where these are missing, is the decision to have an abortion really made in a climate of freedom to choose?

Motherhood

People felt they became adult through having responsibility for others (Barry, 2001). As they got older, they gained practical skills in parenting, domestic work, or budgeting. For some young mothers, parenting did not come naturally and, thrown in at the deep end, they felt the need for training. There were exceptions:

> I just lifted her and held her really close to me and that was just it. And things did come natural, it did in the end, you know – even the simplest things for me, changing the nappy, the feeding, the bathing. It's amazing how quickly it does come to you ... I hear people saying, 'Young people, you know, young mothers, they haven't a clue', and I always say, 'Hold on a wee minute here, anyone having a child, whether they're 35 or 15, is going into it for the first time and none of them have a clue what's ahead of them', you know, it's no different.
> (Quoted in Barry, 2001, p. 38)

The transition to independent adulthood is not necessarily accomplished through motherhood, which might serve the function (to the grandparent) of extending the dependency of the young mother. Tabberer *et al.* (2000) found that, for some young people, motherhood resulted in a reintegration into the family of origin. Their study suggests that parenthood may confirm adulthood rather than confer it. Thus, in the case of one who had already begun to live independently, having the child was a second step which was easier in some ways:

> I think to be honest for a lot of teenage mums the problem is with people asking them. And the reason people didn't ask me was – when I moved in with Julian, I made a big decision, and I proved to my

> parents and my friends I could live like an adult: choose my own paths and make my own decisions. I had to go to loggerheads with a lot of them to get that, and the fact that I made my own decision the first time and proved them wrong, I think a lot of them didn't feel they could push their opinion on me.
> (Cheryl, quoted in Tabberer *et al.*, 2000, p. 34)

There is nevertheless an association between caring for others and perceptions of maturity. This is reflected both in patterns of desistance in criminal careers (Chapter 2 showed how female offenders in particular tended to desist from offending because of relationships) and in the feelings of young people who have caring responsibility for their own parents (see below).

> I think it makes people grow up a lot more. Everybody told me I was really mature anyway, but I think I've grown up a lot more since I had [the baby]. I realise all about looking after kids, you've got to take responsibility for your own family, make sure they are well and I'm not going to go out and get into trouble, and get locked up and for my kids to go into a home. I think it keeps you out of trouble, it stops you from getting into a lot of mess.
> (Quoted in Tabberer *et al.*, 2000, p. 34)

Fatherhood

While the general pattern (among parents of all ages) is for births outside marriage to be jointly registered by both parents, among young parents, births are increasingly registered by the mothers alone (Bynner *et al.*, 2002, forthcoming). It appears that fathers may be taking a less active role. Several projects explored young men's views on teenage pregnancy and parental responsibility:

> In the current political and cultural climate, our response to young, single fathers has been based on a range of assumptions about masculinity, changing male roles and, in relation to the youngest men, media portrayals of feckless youth.
> (Speak *et al.*, 1997, p. 4)

Little is known about the role of young single fathers or the barriers they may have to overcome if they wish to participate in their children's upbringing (Speak *et al.*, 1997). This study of young fathers who wanted to be involved with their children found they were made to feel unimportant both during the pregnancy and after the birth. The men saw 'being there' for their children as important, but felt there was no encouragement other than to contribute financially towards the child's maintenance (the Child Support Act focuses on financial responsibility). Most did not realise that as unmarried fathers they had no legal rights even when their names were on the birth certificate (Pickford, 1999). They felt excluded from support groups for fathers. The attitude of their own parents strongly affected the nature of the relationship with their child.

Young men's views about fatherhood were found to be complex (Tabberer *et al.*, 2000). While most saw fatherhood as involving financial responsibility for the child, they were less likely to take responsibility for the conception. The researchers suggest that young men were often willing to hand over total responsibility for contraception to their girlfriends, feeling thus less culpable in the event of an unwanted pregnancy. It seems that they have little concept of risk. Curiously, Tabberer's study showed that young women themselves sometimes thought the young men to be peripheral to the decision-making process:

> To me, men have some say but not a lot really, they think they've got a big say in it but, they haven't really, not really.
> (Quoted in Tabberer *et al.*, 2000, p. 26)

Boyfriends were often happy to let their girlfriends take the decision to end a pregnancy, but some had strong views, as did some of their parents (one of whom reportedly said: 'if you get rid of that child you are murdering my grandchild').

At this age, young men's social lives may still revolve around their same-sex peers (as McDowell

[2001] found in her study of white working-class young men). Around half went to pubs and clubs at the weekend: ('I'm a bit of a lad, one of the lads, up for a joke, messing about, going out in a group but we don't cause trouble, fight or that', quoted in McDowell, 2001, p. 31). Some had girlfriends ('On Friday I go out with "our lass", and on Saturday it's wi' me mates') and all hoped to become fathers in due course.

The young men tended, however, to have particularly judgemental views about teenage pregnancy, blaming the parents, blaming the young women, but not blaming the young fathers.

> It makes me sick, girls at that age. They have still got their lives to live and you can't live a life with a kid at that age.
> (Quoted in McDowell, 2001, p. 34)

One 'lad' who had been having sex since he was 13, was more cynical and said:

> Well you have got to be careful; you don't just – don't – be stupid. 'Cos you can go to prison for that if you are 16 and the girl is under that. If she presses charges you have lost it 'cos she can press charges and claim money and that. 'Cos you know what girls are like ... They'd do owt for money.
> (Quoted in McDowell, 2001, p. 34)

The role of men in teenage pregnancy and motherhood seems to have been marginalised not only by young people of both sexes, but also in official accounts. Fatherhood, especially absent fatherhood, is reduced to financial responsibility. Some young men seem not even to see themselves as responsible for the conception, and the response of young women is therefore to deny them any say, rather than to encourage them to take an active role. The focus on women's rights over their own bodies, in relation here to abortion or contraception, and their responsibilities as mothers of young children, has perhaps underplayed the *rights and responsibilities* of young men.

Summary

The ways in which young people make their domestic transitions to adulthood are polarising into the majority whose transitions are extended over many years, and a minority whose transitions are rapid, stigmatised and potentially problematic. This polarisation needs to be explained and understood. What was previously a middle-class pattern of extended transition is becoming more widespread among the more affluent working class, and is now a majority pattern. We do not know whether this trend is because people are positively choosing to marry and have children later in their lives, or because lack of resources and the demands of mortgages and expensive lifestyles cause them to defer family building. At the other end of the scale, there is a continuation of working-class patterns of early childbirth, which has become more problematic as the support structures of marriage, job security and formal welfare systems have become eroded.

These slow-track and fast-track patterns are closely linked to socio-economic background and educational level. There are also continuing gender differences. Women typically marry and have children at a lower age than their partners, though this pattern would be expected to change as women's educational levels increase, their attachment to the labour market becomes stronger, and their incomes play a more and more crucial role in their family finances. In the longer term, the trends towards remaining single and childless may constitute a greater problem than teenage pregnancy.

In the interactions between young men and young women, the emphasis appears to be on sexual intercourse and its outcomes, rather than on personal relationships. There is a need for more research to explore how lasting partnerships – leading to shared parenthood – can develop from these rather humble origins. There is no sense, either in these young people's accounts or in official policy reports, of the prospects for fostering positive partnerships around the concept of closeness, intimacy and interdependence. The policy emphasis on teenage *pregnancy* and on fathers' *financial* responsibility may be encouraging this very partial view. This suggests that the policy focus could usefully shift from teenage pregnancy to teenage *parenthood*. The Social Exclusion Unit (1999a) report on *Teenage Pregnancy* recognises that young fathers need to be brought into the picture, but aims to do this through sex and relationships education in school, and through the active pursuit of the Child Support Agency. The possibility that young men could contribute to their children's upbringing *as fathers* appears to be overlooked, as is the possibility that instrumental sexual relationships with girlfriends could lead to more loving relationships over time.

Again, family background is important. Young people's experience of their own parents' relationship and its impact on them as children is likely to influence their expectations of adult life. The ways in which relationships and parenthood are talked about in the family are an important constituent of the family's cultural capital, likely to affect both the behaviour of young people and whether families provide emotional and economic support for domestic transitions. With the withdrawal (or lack) of state support, informal family support has become important for young people needing to set up an independent home, or needing help with child care. Where family support is not forthcoming, there is a need for a clear structure of alternatives – housing, child care and sex and abortion counselling are some examples.

The problem for young people is that society seems to define some patterns of transition as inappropriate and then condemn them, even though they may be based on long-standing class or cultural traditions. There is an expectation that white middle-class patterns should be followed and that alternatives are wrong.

4 Families of origin

We have a responsibility as a Government to help develop rounded individuals who can call on support when they need it, and who can develop their horizons both socially, and in terms of educational and economic expectation and opportunity. The first port of call for support is of course the family, but sometimes parents themselves don't know who to turn to for advice and support for their children.
(DfEE, 2000, p. 5)

[Being a young person here is] *shit, it is shit really. If you haven't been brought up with money ... like a family who can do things and pay for you to do things, then you haven't really got a chance.*
(Holly, quoted in Johnston *et al.*, 2000a, p. 22)

Policy context

The Labour Manifesto describes the new welfare state as 'work for those who can, security for those who cannot' (Labour Party, 2001). Welfare has been replaced by 'workfare' as the work ethic has been reinforced. This policy works better for the adult population than for young people who have not yet entered the world of work.

In response to concerns about the breakdown of family life (see Chapter 3), the government is seeking to support families and reduce child poverty. The Working Families Tax Credit and the move towards implementing EU family-friendly employment practices are all part of this policy thrust. The emphasis, however, is on supporting marriage and the parenting of children. Little attention has been paid to the parenting of young people (Jones and Bell, 2000) and, in consequence, the policy legislation which has extended the period of dependence in youth has not been matched with legislation extending the responsibility of parents.

The policy legislation offers no clear guidelines to parents in the UK on their parental responsibility to young people over the age of 16 years. Even though education and training policies are increasingly defining young people as wholly dependent on their parents until the age of 18 years, there is no explicit provision for this in family policy. Despite the fact that young people are not defined as independent adults until the ages of 21 ('mature students'), 22 (Minimum Wage legislation) or 25 (Income Support, Housing Benefit), and are therefore expected to be dependent on their parents until those ages, in practice they are dependent on a system of moral rather than legal parental obligations. In other words, whether their parents provide economic support for young people over the age of 16 may be dependent on goodwill, the quality of the parent–child relationship and the wealth of the parents. The state may have withdrawn welfare support, but this does not mean that parents have stepped in to fill the gap in the safety net (Jones, 1995; Jones and Bell, 2000).

Changing patterns

Young people's experiences of family life are very varied. Around one in four children born in 1979 was likely to have been affected by divorce by the age of 16; the proportion of dependent children living in lone-parent families has tripled since 1972; it is estimated that over one million children live in stepfamilies; and there are 27,000 children and young people being looked after by local authorities (National Statistics, 2000). For many young people, then, 'parent' might mean a lone parent, an absent parent, a step-parent or a foster parent.

These trends may have affected young people's transitions to adulthood in three different ways. First, if families have become more unstable, it is possible that the intergenerational transmission of both advantage and disadvantage may have weakened, so that it is easier, for example, to overcome the effect of childhood poverty, or to be downwardly mobile intergenerationally. Intergenerational transmission not only of economic capital but also of cultural capital (values such as the work ethic, the education ethic or the family ethic) could be affected. Second, if families have become more dispersed, then kinship networks and systems of kinship obligation may be under threat. This would affect some young people's ability to obtain financial support from their families. Third, it is becoming increasingly difficult to define who the responsible parent is, when family breakdown and reconstitution may leave many parents, including biological ones, uncertain what their continuing parenting roles involve.

JRF research

Although the intergenerational relationship between young people and their parents was the main area of inquiry in only one project (Gillies *et al.*, 2001), the issue kept cropping up in several projects, as the family context in which young people play out their transitions to adulthood has become more important. This chapter first draws on quantitative research to see whether intergenerational transmission of advantage and disadvantage has increased, and whether education really does have an intervening effect. It then discusses the findings from qualitative projects that explored aspects of the relationship between young people and their parents. It examines some of the ways in which parents can help their adult children and ease their transitions to adulthood. It concludes with an exploration of the findings from projects that turn the notions of dependence and independence on their heads: studies of young people with disabilities, young people who care for their parents and young people who are looked after by their local authorities.

Intergenerational transmission of (dis)advantage

Studies have shown that family poverty has increased over the last few decades. Children are more likely to be growing up in households where neither parent is in full-time work, and more likely to be living on a low household income. The Family Expenditure Survey indicates that, in 1997, 25 per cent of households were living in poverty. In seeking to tackle poverty, the government has placed a significant emphasis on the value of education. The question that arises is whether education can intervene to overcome early family disadvantage, or whether family poverty is transmitted into the next generation. Several studies, including Bynner *et al.* (2002, forthcoming), suggest that family background continues to be a critical factor in its influence on educational attainment.

In a meritocracy that invests in extending education and widening access, family background should become less relevant than individual ability. Abigail McKnight (Bynner *et al.*, 2002, forthcoming) explored whether the association between childhood poverty and disadvantage in adult life had changed over time, by comparing data from the 1958 and 1970 birth cohorts. The economic status and earnings of young adults who grew up in low-income households are compared with those who grew up in higher-income households. Both cohort data sets show that above-average household income at age 16 increases the likelihood of a young adult being in employment and being in a better-paid job. However, the association between childhood poverty and *both* low-paid work *and* unemployment in adulthood has become stronger. For some, it remains difficult to escape early disadvantage.

Family background affects life chances (educational attainment, labour market attachment and earnings), and there is evidence that this 'poverty penalty' has increased over time:

> *The current emphasis on the role of educational attainment in shaping individuals' working lives has put greater pressure on young people and encouraged parents to direct resources at enabling their children to achieve within the educational system. Longer transitions between school and work are likely to create an additional financial burden on parents. If the cost of assisting young people into 'good jobs' has increased over time the link between parental income and labour market success may have strengthened.*
> (Bynner *et al.*, 2002, forthcoming)

We have already seen in Chapter 2 how parents have not necessarily taken on board this encouragement to underwrite their children's education (Forsyth and Furlong, 2000). This is one reason why individuals from higher-income households are still more than three times as likely to obtain a degree than individuals from poor households, while those from poor households make up a disproportionate number of those with no qualifications at all. Another reason is poverty itself. In fact, the research of Bynner *et al.* (2002, forthcoming) shows that, in terms of employment prospects (earnings, levels of employment), 'the penalty of growing up in low-income households has increased over time', even when education is controlled for. The study found that education was 'not enough', and that family poverty must be addressed, if the 'cycle of deprivation' is to be broken:

> *The rise in the proportion of children growing up in poverty is alarming, not just because of the disadvantages these children inevitably suffer in their childhood, but because they carry this disadvantage into their adult working lives.*
> (Bynner *et al.*, 2002, forthcoming)

Inequalities in parental wealth are therefore a cause for concern. Several of the studies found

evidence of a continuing effect of family economic circumstances on later outcomes. Parents' social class, level of education, experience of unemployment, housing situations and other indicators of advantage and disadvantage differentially affected whether a young person stayed on in education, achieved a degree, experienced unemployment (Forsyth and Furlong, 2000; Dolton *et al.*, 1999; Stafford *et al.*, 1999). Dolton *et al.* (1999) found, however, that disadvantaged family background had a less detrimental effect on women than on men, if education intervened. In other words, education 'worked' better for women in redressing existing disadvantage.

Family relationships

Qualitative studies of young people and their families of origin can help explain why intergenerational transmission – of economic and cultural capital – works. The first issue to address is the quality of the relationship between young people and their parents.

There has been very little research on the relationship between young people and their parents, and the focus has been on problematic aspects, or on unemployed or homeless young people in working-class families. Some studies touched on the subject indirectly. The Teesside study, for example, found that, although some young people had positive (and protective) relationships with both their parents, mothers were mentioned more frequently than fathers, and for others more problematic relationships resulting from a father being in prison, or drug addiction in the family, had a direct effect on offending behaviour in youth (Johnston *et al.*, 2000a). Several of the young working-class men in McDowell's (2001) study admired their fathers and described close relationships with them (which included having a drink or going fishing together), although two fathers were reported to drink too much. Some expressed a determination not to become like their fathers. Their relations with their mothers on the other hand were largely based on domestic support: 'I get my meals and everything done for me' (quoted in McDowell, 2001, p. 33).

McDowell found that family circumstances were important but the effects were unpredictable – divorce and separation, death, physical violence, drug and alcohol abuse affected some but not others. On the other hand (Johnston *et al.*, 2000a), particular key experiences including bereavement and loss could be significant and could precipitate or facilitate the termination of criminality, for example. Britton *et al.* (2002, forthcoming) found that traumatic events at home were not responded to, or probably even known about, in schools, and so young people in need of a lifeline were not offered one.

A study by Smith *et al.* (1998) of the relationship between homeless young people and their parents found that most of the former had left home at 16 or 17 years, often after conflict between their parents and/or domestic violence. Disagreements between young people and their parents also led to leaving home: in the case of young women these arose because of boyfriends, while in the case of young men they were more likely to be about school behaviour, drug-taking or trouble with the police. There were also disagreements over levels of board money, which according to the young people were sometimes set unrealistically high in relation to their income levels.

Acting as a counterbalance to this research, one project by Jane Ribbens and her colleagues studied 'ordinary young people and their families' (Gillies *et al.*, 2001). Most of the sample[1] described positive relationships which improved with age, sometimes becoming more companionate. Parents often provided practical support, passing on knowledge and experience, offering advice. There was support through important transitions, such as subsidising through university, or driving to a job interview. Most young people in the study saw their mothers in particular as concerned and caring, and their

fathers as more protective (and sometimes angry). Some found themselves growing apart from their fathers as they grew older. For most parents:

> ... parent–teenager relationships were experienced in terms of enduring responsibility, love and interdependence. The accounts ... were certainly not predominantly stories of stress and difficulty in living with teenagers: indeed, they give the contrasting message that being the parent of a teenager is not necessarily as difficult as we might be led to expect.
> (Gillies *et al.*, 2001, p. 8)

The research explored the extent of shared experience and beliefs among young people and their parents. They discussed three main themes, as follows.

Independence and relatedness

Both parents and teenagers portrayed earning money and passing exams, and leaving home, as particularly significant moves towards fully 'independent adulthood' (Gillies *et al.*, 2001). Though some young people experienced independence negatively in terms of disconnection and isolation from their families, the majority saw independence as:

> ... signifying a new liberty to act as an individual, but also as obligating them to account for the consequences of these individual actions.
> (Gillies *et al.*, 2001, p. 14)

Other parents felt that the emancipation of their teenage children brought with it entitlement to a new phase of 'life of their own', though the closeness continued.

The concept of support

It can be difficult for both parents and their adolescent children to find the right balance of support and independence in this relationship (Finch, 1989). Some parents in the Gillies *et al.* (2001) study were more directive than others. One mother said 'I feel as though I'm still trying to manipulate his life in a way that he comes out alright', and a father said 'I'm still a bit of a dictator', while other parents were less directive ('You sort of advise instead of telling'). The young people, needing space in which to make decisions, appreciated in particular the approval and encouragement of their parents. (See also Hendey and Pascall, 2002, on this issue with regard to disabled young people.)

The meaning of 'family'

There was a strong consensus that 'families' meant units, in which values and experiences were shared, characterised by closeness and belonging, loving relationships and a shared responsibility (see also Morrow, 1998, on children's perceptions of family). The ethos of 'family' can thus be transferred from generation to generation. These ideals were not always matched with reality, however. While most took it for granted that their parents loved and worried about them, and would always 'be there' for them, others, without parental support, drew on resources outside the family, including friendships and professional help (alternative support). In three cases, young people said there was no concern, commitment or emotional attachment with their parents:

> *She never treated me like a mother should treat a daughter, and so I hated her. I didn't love her at all. And I think that if I didn't get away when I did, then I would have ended up to be a really horrible child, you know. Because she didn't have any respect for me basically. All she cared about was her drink.*
> (Quoted in Gillies *et al.*, 2001, p. 20)

Family support

The removal of welfare benefits and student grants and the inadequacy of the Minimum Wage legislation for young people all mean that families have become more important as a resource for young people on low incomes, or struggling to find a niche in the labour or housing markets. It is ironic that families have become more crucial in the lives of young people at a time when 'the family' is seen as under threat. The consequence of government policies may be to put more pressure on those families that are already at risk (Jones and Bell, 2000).

There is ample evidence in the projects that the bereavement and loss associated with family breakdown or the death of a parent affected levels of support. Compared with national statistics, a high proportion of the Teesside sample was or had been living with a lone parent, and 10 per cent had experienced the death of a parent, sibling, partner or child. Other studies showed the importance of a stable family background, and the adverse effects of family breakdown, parental divorce, bereavement and other circumstances that might affect the strength of kinship networks.

The dispersal of families, whether because of marital breakdown or migration, affects kinship supportive networks. An earlier study[2] found that, although contact with relatives has decreased overall, young parents rely on relatives to provide financial help in times of need more than they did a decade ago, while friends were more likely to be relied on for emotional support (McGlone *et al.*, 1998).

There is a conflict between the apparent expectation of policy makers and the expectations of parents about the extent of parental responsibility. A pilot study of family support for young people showed wide variation of patterns among poorer families and the problems experienced by those whose families did not 'rally round' when they needed help (Jones, 1995). Smith *et al.* (1998) compared the background and attitudes of young homeless people with those of other families on a council estate, and found that some parents in both groups believed that their legal responsibilities ceased at age 16.

*She chucked me sister out at 16, me brother, first, at
16. Me Dad said 'You're next, don't worry about it'. I
didn't believe him ... just got kicked out.*
(Quoted in Smith *et al.*, 1998, p. 26)

Positive relationships with parents and kin can
be important to smooth the paths of transition. The
responsibilities of family members towards one
another are the product of private systems of
obligation, negotiated within families and to a great
extent dependent on the quality of family
relationships (Finch, 1989). Parental encouragement
to stay on in education or to get a job depends both
on local traditions and on family belief in the
education ethic or the work ethic. McDowell (2001)
comments on the impact of local traditions and
attitudes on young men's decisions, and on the
importance of informal contacts (being 'spoken for'
by employed male kin) for gaining work. Pavis *et
al.* (2000) found that informal networks were the
key to securing work and housing in rural Scotland
(see also Chapter 2). Rugg and Jones (1999)
comment on the importance of kinship links in
helping to find employment and housing in rural
areas of England.

Help with transport, education and children
There are particular times when parental help is
needed, and this may take the form of practical
help with setting up home (helping move furniture,
decorating, etc.), or financial help to go on a course
(such as paying HE fees and ongoing maintenance),
and providing emotional support during difficult
times, such as pregnancy.

Storey and Brannen (2000) describe the
dependence of young people living in the
countryside on their parents for help with
transport. Not all families had the resources to be
able to provide help with transport. Where
resources existed, help had to be negotiated
between young people and their parents. This was
not always easy. Dependency on lift-giving
provided parents with control over young people's

behaviour. Asking for help may involve a loss of
autonomy (Jones, 1995): thus dependence on kin
and friends for baby-sitting means having to fit in
(Rugg and Jones, 1999). Calling on family
obligations is difficult for both young people and
their parents:

*You don't ask ... 'cos mum might feel she had to do it,
in case she'd be letting you down, even if she didn't
want to.*
(Quoted in Storey and Brannen, 2000, p. 16)

Support for students entering HE may depend
on both the level of cultural capital in the home and
the financial circumstances of parents.
Encouragement to stay in education was found to
depend in part on the educational level of parents.
While nearly all parents approved of their son or
daughter entering HE, there was less agreement
about financial support. Provision of a home was
one of the main forms of parental support, and for
students (cf. workers) this could be free. Though a
majority of parents were willing to provide a high
level of support if their child entered HE, many felt
that they were unable to do so (Forsyth and
Furlong, 2000).

Parents play an important part in the
transmission of family values and beliefs (cultural
capital), as Gillies *et al.* (2001) found. Parental views
on motherhood and abortion were important
factors in determining the decision whether to
continue with a pregnancy or have an abortion.
Family support during the critical period may be
particularly important in the face of local pressures
and prevalent anti-abortion views. Interestingly,
women who became pregnant were often able to
rebuild relationships with their own parents. Smith
et al. (1998) report a young homeless woman as
saying:

*I wanted to get pregnant so I could just move back
home ... 'Cos I missed me mum and dad that much.*
(Smith *et al.*, 1998, p. 36)

The promise of family support helped one young women opt to have her baby:

> If my Mum and Dad said they wouldn't support me I think that would have changed my mind, because I wouldn't have been able to afford to look after her.
> (Quoted in Tabberer et al., 2000, p. 24)

Britton et al. (2002, forthcoming) comment that the young mothers in their sample needed support to balance their parental responsibilities with their (almost universal) wish to be able to get back to their studies, take courses or find employment. However, one young woman was forced by her mother to choose between her family and her baby, and chose the former, having an abortion:

> So I did the worst thing I could do and chose family, and like, a few months after, I ended up in care – so I wish I'd never.
> (Quoted in Tabberer et al., 2000, p. 35)

Parents were often hesitant about giving specific advice, preferring to offer general support (see Gillies et al., 2001). The acceptance of support also has its price, since it implies a resumption or continuation of dependence on parents (Jones, 1995). Tabberer et al. (2000) found that the family could 'capture' the baby, integrating it into their existing families. This was viewed with ambivalence by the young women:

> ... for some young people teenage pregnancy might not represent a move away from the family but a re-integration within it at the same time as other teenagers might be forming their own identities outside the home.
> (Tabberer et al., 2000, p. 33)

Alternative 'dependencies'

While the normative model of transition involves the move from childhood dependence to adult independence, some groups of young people experience rather different types of youth. Research on the transitions of young carers showed how responsibility for others could start very early in life, while research on young people with disabilities showed the struggle to achieve even the smallest degree of independence. Young people in the care of the local authority may have very different experience and expectations of 'dependence' compared with those living with their biological parents.

Growing up caring

Some studies challenge the policy assumption that young people can be dependent on their parents by showing cases where it is the parents who are the dependants and the young people the carers. Several young respondents had coped with a parent on drink or drugs. Some young people have a great deal of family responsibility during their youth and they feel adult as a result. Barry (2001, p. 15) quotes a 16 year old who said:

> There is a lot of pain for me with my [foster] mum, as well. I didn't mention, but she used to be an alcoholic. She used to beat me repeatedly every time she was drunk ... I had to take her home a lot. [At what age?] Eleven, twelve. That's when I started looking after her instead of getting beat up.

Another who had looked after his brother and sister said: 'I think being responsible for other people makes you grow up quicker'. Some felt that the caring responsibility gave them a status that they would otherwise have lacked, but others thought they had had to grow up too quickly:

> I didn't feel like I had all my childhood, because I had to grow up really quick and I had to support my mam through all this, and I saw some bad things that I never want anyone to see.
> (Barry, 2001, p. 31)

> I think I've been an adult all my life.
> (Barry, 2001, p. 33)

The notion that children can be the carers and responsible for others clashes with the prevailing concept of the child as dependent and the recipient of care. In such cases, the normative understanding that parents care for their young until they are ready to become independent adults, as described above, is turned on its head. Extensive research has been undertaken at Loughborough University on the role that children often have as carers for parents with a long-term illness or disability. This study (Dearden and Becker, 2000) of 60 young carers examined how they made the transition to adulthood, in circumstances very different from the norm. Since illness and disability are often associated with poverty, the 'responsibility' to care may lie with children by default, *in the absence of supportive services*, or other family carers. Half of the young carers were living in lone-parent families, where there was no other adult to take on the role (though the presence of a second adult does not necessarily help where they are working, or where the illness is so severe that every family member is expected to help). Family structure, the severity and nature of parental illness, and the availability of other avenues of support determined the level and type of support provided by the young people.

> I missed school a lot because he [dad] wasn't well, and I didn't like leaving him in case he fell over and he couldn't reach a phone or pull the cords.
> (Quoted in Dearden and Becker, 2000, p. 21)

In many cases, then, the role of carer devolved to the child as a result of, and compounding, multiple disadvantage. Dearden and Becker found that many young carers had educational problems and missed school, and consequently failed to achieve any qualifications. This, combined with ongoing caring responsibilities, excluded some from the labour market. While some continued into further education, caring responsibilities in the home made it difficult for some to seek part-time work while studying, thus compounding financial hardship. The normative transition from school into work and away from the family was thus not followed. Leaving home was problematic and some delayed leaving, while the stress where a parent had a severe and enduring mental health problem led some young people to leave home prematurely:

> Things had been going bad for about ten months with my mum's health problems. I was getting to the stage where I knew if I stayed there I would end up ending my life, never mind hers.
> (Quoted in Dearden and Becker, 2000, p. 33)

On the other hand, the kinds of practical skills associated with independence were gained early:

> I think I sort of became an adult when I were fifteen in that way ... like a woman might be running a house, I were doing all the things maybe a twenty-two or -three year old would be doing. I think I became mature when I were fifteen.
> (Quoted in Dearden and Becker, 2000, p. 41)

Disabled young people

Conversely, Hendey and Pascall's (2002) study looked at the problems of young people with disability whose dependence seemed to obstruct their transitions to adulthood. People with profound impairments need to rely a great deal on their own and their families' resources, and many parents fought and negotiated for their children while also ensuring that they could care, fight and negotiate for themselves. Respondents with jobs and independent households most often named parents as the key to their achievements. For some, though, the very closeness of family relationships could be a hindrance to establishing independent living while for others, families could be damaging. Hendey and Pascall argue that the policy emphasis on family responsibility has resulted in a lack of alternative support for those who need it:

They find me difficult to live with – the reality of having a disabled member of the family. They keep implying that I'm stupid, I never do anything for myself, all I do is cause work for them. I feel very unloved.
(Quoted in Hendey and Pascall, 2002, p. 24)

Bignall and Butt (2000) studied the views of young black and Asian disabled people on independent living. The majority had specific goals they wanted to achieve and were actively working towards them. Most relied on their family for care and support, and many were lonely. For some young people, there were difficulties in participating in their own culture, because their own first language was English or British Sign Language, or because their impairment prevented their involvement in religious practices. Independence meant having choice and control in their lives, and this was as important to them as where they lived.

Summary

Many of the studies in the programme showed the significance of the family of origin: in transmitting cultural capital, for example in transferring beliefs about the ethos of education, work or family to the younger generation, and encouraging them to continue in education or to work. Values and beliefs are passed from generation to generation through family life. One of the reasons why the educational level of parents affects the educational level of their children is that parents differentially transmit a belief in the value of education to their children. The intergenerational transmission of beliefs may be as important as that of economic disadvantage in creating the pattern whereby teenage parenthood is intergenerationally reproduced.

Parents are also essential providers of economic capital, providing financial support for their adult children to help them pay the costs of courses, or parenthood, or a home. The studies showed that access to these forms of help varied, and that many young people were without family support. In such circumstances, it was important that alternative means of support be present, but with the withdrawal of the state safety net this was not the case. Family economic circumstances and family relationships are important factors in determining whether young people can gain access to family help or not. Families may not be able to support their adult children or they may not be willing to. As in other areas of young people's lives, there is a polarisation of experience between those who received help from their families and those who did not. The latter are dependent on an inadequate system of state benefits which are not geared to support the transition to adulthood.

Finally, the model of youth as being essentially a period of transition from being a dependent child to being an independent adult is severely tested by some of the projects. Other research has indicated that interdependence between young people and their parents is a common feature of family life. Children's contributions to the household may be undervalued or may even go unnoticed. Equally, the continuing need for dependence of some young people may be overlooked if we expect that, when youth is completed, independent adulthood has been achieved. Young people interpret independent citizenship in different ways, as the next chapter will show.

5 Independence and citizenship

For most young people, adulthood brings a degree of autonomy, the capacity to make decisions for oneself, the opportunity to gain economic independence, responsibility for others, and the chance to gain from and contribute to the wider society. The transition to independence is one of the main dynamics during the period of youth, though it is gained in different ways. Independence, the capacity for informed choice, empowerment and participation are themes which run through many of the projects in the programme. The ways young people talk about independence and citizenship sometimes run counter to the 'official view', embodied in policy. It is therefore important to understand young people's own constructions.

This penultimate chapter describes the findings of the projects in relation to independence and citizenship. It summarises what these terms mean for young people in different circumstances, drawing together some of the findings from previous chapters. It then considers the rhetoric about active participation, for example in political processes, and considers who participates and whether participation gives any real power to effect change. It considers also some research which has actively involved young people in the research process. Finally, it questions whether 'citizenship' in these terms can have any real meaning for young people when they are excluded from economic participation. As before, though, we start with a brief review of the policy context.

The policy context

Young people are not full citizens of society, because they do not have direct access to the citizenship rights of adults, but nor do they have indirect rights as children do, via their parents or carers. This puts young people in a particularly anomalous position vis-à-vis the state, and helps to 'explain' why it is difficult for policy makers to create structures that can really address the

problems that young people face. They have to decide whether to support young people directly or whether to provide financial incentives to their parents to support them (Jones and Bell, 2000). Chapter 4 showed how variable was the practice of family support and parental awareness of their role in mediating between young people and the state.

In policy terms, young people cannot become full adult citizens until they reach their mid-20s. Access to welfare benefits and the right to work are being withheld from them. Nevertheless, there is a prevailing rhetoric about citizenship – the need to provide citizenship education, to encourage young people to undertake voluntary work, and so on (Jones and Bell, 2000). This particular facet of citizenship bears little relation to the notion developed by T.H. Marshall as an underlying tenet of the post-war welfare state, which defined citizenship in terms of civil, political and social rights (1952). In current policy terms, citizenship is constructed by the current Labour government as a package of rights and responsibilities in which the former are dependent on the latter – to put it another way, you have to put something into the system before you can get something from it. Among adults, this means contributing as a taxpayer. Full participation in society is the reward for work.

This view is problematic when applied to young people, whose opportunities to contribute formally to society are limited: they are either in education, or on low incomes, or both. The age at which young people gain access to full-time employment has continually increased. We have seen in Chapter 2 how young people's constructions of 'work' are very varied, ranging from academic study to formal employment in the labour market, to caring for relatives and including (for some) criminal activity. The prevailing construction of work in policy terms, however, tends to be restricted to labour market activity. Unfortunately for young people, however positive their contributions – for example to school/college work, or to helping in the home or family business – these do not count towards recognition as an independent citizen. It is not young people's own constructions that matter to policy makers, but a normative ideal:

> We want a literate, numerate, but also civilised society in which actively contributing to the well-being of others is seen as a natural part of a strong and caring community.
> (David Blunkett, DfEE Press Release 104/99)

Definitions of (in)dependence

Young people define independence in different ways. In contrast to the philosophy underlying welfare policies and the stress on 'welfare dependency', or dependence on the state, young people see their dependence and independence mainly in relation to their parents. In their constructions they refer to developing autonomy and responsibility. Young people in the Gillies *et al.* (2001) study variously described independence in terms of autonomy (the ability to take some responsibility for one's own actions, often in relation to going out at night), responsibility for others, individuality (of personality) and the ability to cope alone (particularly among those who had personal or family problems). Becoming independent therefore is most usually associated with emancipation from parental authority and detachment from the parental home.

However, in parallel with developing responsibility, there is the notion of developing economic independence. The two go hand in hand. Most young people attach overwhelming importance to the economic independence afforded by a well-paid job, while some see the move away from the parental home as a significant step towards independence. Specifically, both parents and teenagers portrayed earning money, passing exams and leaving home as particularly significant

moves towards fully 'independent adulthood' (Gillies *et al.*, 2001, p. 17).

The research in the programme as a whole suggests that, when one facet of independence is not available, another gets stressed. Thus, for those who are unable to work because of disabilities, other forms of independence become important means of empowerment.

Some research indicates that independence has its downside, as Chapter 4 showed. Gillies *et al.* (2001) indicated that learning to cope alone was a significant aspect of independence particularly for those with personal or family problems. The research by Save the Children Fund (Barry, 2001) found that young people who lacked a caring parent and had to take responsibility for themselves, learning to 'cope to survive', thought they had become independent too early in their lives. Similarly, research by Dearden and Becker (2000) on those who had been caring for a parent with a disability showed the extent to which some children have responsibilities far beyond what might be expected for their age:

> When you're young like that, you shouldn't have to be independent at that age.
> (Quoted in Barry, 2001, p. 31)

Reconstructing autonomy

In some circumstances, economic independence and responsibility for others become difficult to achieve. Hendey and Pascall (2002) show how disabled young people overcome the barriers to living fully independent social and economic lives, and are still able to develop a sense of themselves as citizens, either through their relationship to the state welfare system as 'beneficiaries', or as contributors through voluntary work. The authors comment that it was perhaps the stigma of the former which led to a strong desire to contribute something to society. For the black and Asian disabled people studied by Bignall and Butt (2000),

6 Implications for policy

This final chapter considers the implications of the programme findings for youth policies. Each of the preceding chapters has concluded with a summary, and so there is no need to repeat those here. Instead, the chapter aims to evaluate some of the problems with current policies for young people and to put forward some suggestions for a new approach to policy thinking. In the second part of the chapter, separate areas of policy – not necessarily relating to separate government departments – are then addressed and some specific policy recommendations are made. These recommendations are framed in relation to existing areas of concern among policy makers and represent an attempt to synthesise the main recommendations of individual projects.

Revising approaches to research and policy

If policies for young people are to be effective, then the whole policy approach to the age group needs to be brought under scrutiny. Currently, too many policies are based on outdated and false assumptions about 'youth', too few take real account of the family context of young people's lives and the current emphasis on targeting fails to address the needs of the many who risk falling through the gaps in the safety net (by focusing on those who have already fallen through).

Abandoning outdated normative assumptions
Policies for young people need to move on from their dependence on the normative transitions of the past. Jones and Bell (2000) define the underlying and outdated assumptions that have guided government thinking for too long, as:

- *age*: where there are expectations clearly defined in legislation that people gain competence with age, regardless of social class, gender, or cultural variation

- *dependency*: that young people can remain dependent on their parents for longer and longer periods

- *parenting*: that parents will accept responsibility for their children until they are in their mid-20s

- *economic rationality*: that economic criteria govern decision making, so that economic incentives or disincentives can be effectively employed to control behaviour

- *empowerment*: that 'giving young people a voice', or inviting them to participate, confers power on them

- *conformity*: that young people will sign up to white middle-class conventional aspirations.

Underlying many of these is the assumption that young people constitute a problem for the rest of society. This commonly held view overlooks the very real problems that society, and social policies, present to young people. It can be used to justify the lack of adequate social protection for young people, and it can stem from a lack of respect for them (Jones and Bell, 2000). In consequence, young people are seen as responsible for the difficulties they get into, such as teenage pregnancy, homelessness, joblessness, debt and poverty. Policies should be more sensitive to variations in youth in terms both of problems and of solutions.

Extending the holistic approach
There is greater awareness in policy circles of the need for joined-up policies. The research programme provides further evidence of the need to continue this process. Holistic policies for young people would need to take into account the different contexts in which they are becoming adult: in particular their life course and family contexts.

Life course context

In both research and policy, there is a tendency to define 'youth' as a distinct entity, a clearly defined stage of the life course, for which policy initiatives can be targeted. This is to deny that the period of youth, however defined in terms of age, is preceded by childhood and followed by adulthood, in a continuous life course context.

It is important to recognise the significance during youth of earlier life experiences. Much research has indicated the continuing significance of childhood poverty, or childhood loss and bereavement, for later outcomes, including truancy and disaffection with school (e.g. Bynner *et al.*, 2002, forthcoming; Dolton *et al.*, 1999). The research has also suggested that supportive interventions in childhood might help to mitigate the effects of childhood disadvantage. Equally, research has noted that disadvantage during youth, such as early experience of unemployment, can have a damaging effect on later earnings and attachment to the labour market (Bynner *et al.*, 2002, forthcoming). Again, interventions can help. It is important not to 'write off' social groups who are seen to be problematic for society, but to recognise that appropriate interventions can have an effect in the longer as well as the shorter term.

Family context

In both research and policy, there has been a focus on the individual. The emphasis on individual transitions should not neglect the social context in which transitions are made. It was a failing for many years in youth studies to pay little attention to young people's families, despite the fact that for most people the family home is the launching pad for adult life. The significance of family life and family relationships comes out strongly in this research programme. There are indications that there is insufficient awareness in the formal institutions of schools or social services of the variations in family patterns of care and support. In particular, the research has identified areas where

family support needs to be supplemented with alternative provisions. There needs to be closer collaboration between those formulating youth policies and those formulating family policies.

Recognising the problems of targeting

Policies tend to focus on poor neighbourhoods as a practical means of targeting socially excluded young people. The Connexions Service for 13–19 year olds, while presented as a provision for all young people, specifically aims to provide a 'ladder out of social exclusion' for individuals by 'breaking the cycle of non-participation and under-achievement'. This is to be achieved through personal advisers (Connexions, 2000). For the strategy to work, it will be necessary to track young people so that they do not drop out of the system, but two projects in the JRF programme (Britton *et al.*, 2002; Johnston *et al.*, 2000a) have indicated that tracking will be difficult. Johnston and his colleagues have other misgivings: they warn that advisers may experience tension between their official roles and the need to support young people who may 'break the rules'; that reaching the most excluded young people will involve the kinds of skills previously associated with detached youth work; that there needs to be flexibility about the age range, so that under-13s and over-19s can receive support if they need it; and that Connexions may appear irrelevant in the most deprived areas.

'Poor neighbourhoods'

The problem of whether to target specific neighbourhoods is not an easy one. On the one hand, labour market economists would argue (as Dolton *et al.*, 1999 do) that local labour market conditions are influential and that increased funding (e.g. for education) for disadvantaged local authorities and depressed regions would have a direct effect on the labour market prospects of these areas. On the other hand, some research has indicated that poor neighbourhoods are not homogeneous, even though they are treated as such. Because social inequalities exist within communities, some people are more able to overcome community disadvantage than others. There are therefore dangers in focusing on communities, as targeted interventions may only help those who would have 'achieved' without them and fail to address the problems of others more in need. Thus, Forsyth and Furlong (2000) do not consider that initiatives to increase HE quotas on a community level will be effective, as this will benefit only the advantaged minority in such areas. It is therefore important to recognise the variation in circumstances and responses among residents of inner-city neighbourhoods (Johnston *et al.*, 2000a) or, equally, of deprived rural areas (Rugg and Jones, 1999):

> If youth policy is to be effective it needs a clear, sociological understanding of the local conditions and cultures that generate the different ways in which young people get by in socially excluded areas.
> (Johnston et al., 2000b, p. 4)

'The socially excluded'

It is tempting, when so many studies identify a minority cluster at the bottom of the socio-economic heap, to want to focus on this group. After all, 'they' are the ones who do not subscribe to the education ethic, truanting and failing to obtain the qualifications that 'they' will need; 'they' are the ones most likely to become unemployed in adulthood, or be in low-paid jobs; 'they' are the ones who become teenage parents; 'they' are the ones who leave home 'too soon' and become homeless. 'They' are fairly easy to identify and, if they cannot be 'saved' and become full participants in society, then they will pass on their disadvantage to their children, and their children's children.

If only it were as simple as that. The research shows an association between these different facets of disadvantage and exclusion, through statistical analysis of large data sets, and it also shows examples of multiple disadvantage, through local

case studies, *but it does not show the nature of the link.* We cannot assume that there is a static and homogeneous group of multiply disadvantaged young people who can be targeted for interventions. Even if there were, this 20 per cent, or 10 per cent, would only be the visible tip of an iceberg. Many other young people would risk joining their group. Furthermore, young people's lives can change very rapidly and individuals can move in and out of visibly excluded groups (Britton *et al.*, 2002, forthcoming). It is therefore important that 'the disadvantaged' are not stereotyped and stigmatised, and that the wider problems of young people are also addressed.

Towards an agenda for effective policies

Many of the projects described in this report put forward recommendations for policy and practice. By synthesising the findings here, clear messages come across, with some specific implications for policy and practice. In a number of policy areas, ideas about how to improve policy and provision have been proposed by the researchers, and these are now presented.

Extending education take-up

Education is seen as the principal means to overcome poverty and disadvantage, and, perhaps more significantly in the current policy agenda, as a means of validating social inclusion and full social participation.

For the expansion of education to be effective, young people and their families need to be persuaded to take up education and training opportunities rather than try to enter the impoverished youth labour market. The curriculum should be readdressed, since secondary education higher qualifications are currently geared to university entry (rather than entry into the labour market) and may be outdated (Bynner *et al.*, 2002, forthcoming). The issue of bias on the grounds of social class, gender, ethnicity, disability and community should be addressed in schools and colleges. Selling the idea of education also requires a shift in the educational ethos of many families (and schools). New ways must be found to address disaffected young men when they are still at school and inform them of the realities of the labour market (McDowell, 2001). This could take the form of peer education by 18–20 year olds with labour market experience, or a 'school into work' programme in the final compulsory school year (Lloyd, 1999). The message is that Education Maintenance Allowances and other financial incentives to stay in education cannot work on their own. If educational aspirations are to be raised, there is also a case for educating the parents of young people and encouraging them to gain educational qualifications (Stafford et al., 1999) through Lifelong Learning initiatives.

The notion that 'Higher Education is good for you' should not be followed unthinkingly, when there remain many obstacles in a system supposedly based on academic merit. There is a need to question 'levels of participation' in HE (Forsyth and Furlong, 2000), and the impact higher levels will have on standards and outcomes. The earnings and status value of a degree is likely to continue to reduce, and student debt increase, as more young people stay on. The issue of student finance should be addressed again: fees should be abolished and non-returnable bursaries or grants reintroduced for poorer students. These should be supplemented with better-quality, low-cost student accommodation and assistance with travel. Student loans should not be based on the premise that graduates earn more.

Labour market

Even if extended education is desirable for (if not desired by) all, there will still be young people who enter the labour market and who need jobs. Whatever the inducement to lure young people

into staying on in the education and training system, there are some who seek to enter 'a highly competitive labour market' and risk unemployment (Bynner et al., 2002, forthcoming). Although for 18–24 year olds there is the New Deal, there remains something of a gap in provision for 16/17 year olds, who are not covered by National Minimum Wage legislation or Income Support. The youth labour market may be phasing out but it still needs support and young workers still need protection.

There needs to be an easier transition from education into the labour market, especially for earlier school leavers. The links between education and labour market institutions need to be improved (McDowell, 2001). Young people need an extended period of support in the first steps towards employment, and employers should take on the task of vocational training for all young people entering their first jobs (Bynner et al., 2002, forthcoming). Young people in disadvantaged areas need better-paid jobs which they can use as stepping stones into the adult labour market, and these need to be created.

Simply having a job is not enough (Pavis et al., 2000) as young people in low-paid and low-quality employment still felt undervalued and marginalised in their communities. Interventions are needed to alter the terms and conditions of low-paid work (McDowell, 2001), and young people's earnings should be reviewed. The transitional National Minimum Wage should be abolished and all over-18s should be entitled to the adult rate. There is an urgent need for help with transport costs, especially for those in rural areas, to break the 'no car, no job' cycle. Perhaps this could be met by the Access Fund under the Investing in Young People strategy, or through the Youth Cards? A mobility grant in rural areas would allow young people to access wider education and training opportunities (Shucksmith, 2000).

Reducing teenage pregnancies

One of the main reasons why teenage pregnancy is seen as a problem (other than under-16 pregnancies) is that they tend to lead to lone parenthood and poverty. Policies to address teenage pregnancy need to seek ways not only of reducing conceptions and providing support for young mothers, but also of engaging young fathers in the role of partners and parents.

The main focus is still on educational provision in schools, but this should be extended to include more relationship education. Abortion information should be included in sex education (Tabberer *et al.*, 2000). The recent misguided and unrealistic government sex education programme aimed at discouraging sexual activity among young people should have focused instead on preventing pregnancy though contraception.

Young mothers need an effective and widespread system of child care to enable them to work if they wish, wherever they live. They should not have to be dependent on informal systems of child care, or on family obligations. The New Deal for Lone Parents caters for mothers over 18 years, but younger mothers may also need alternative provision ranging from child care to supported accommodation. Care should, however, be taken to support positive relationships between young mothers and their partners where appropriate and not to cause them to separate.

Young men seem to miss out on health, relationship and sex education. They need advice about sex, from an impersonal source, as well as help in dealing with issues of violence and abuse in the home (McDowell, 2001). Agencies should address the needs of young fathers, in terms of education for parenthood, counselling and support. Parenthood education work undertaken in young offenders' institutions provides a model for what other agencies could achieve (Speak *et al.*, 1997). The current emphasis on the financial responsibility of absent fathers is misleading and

should be accompanied by a reinforcement of the wider concept of parental responsibility. Health education should also be targeted at young men (Stafford *et al.*, 1999).

Housing and homelessness

There is still a heavy policy reliance on parents for accommodation, despite the fact that young people may need to leave home (Jones, 1995; Rugg, 1999). However, if young people are to live at home beyond the age of 16, their financial needs must be recognised: 16–18s in particular (especially those whose parents do not receive Child Benefit for them) should receive an income that enables them to pay board money to their parents. EMA may be sufficient to permit this for some young people, but it is very targeted, and the levels of allowance received by most people would not be adequate. The alternative would be to extend Child Benefit to cover all under-18s living in the parental home.

Supplementing family care

The programme findings suggest that the shift of responsibility from the state to the family has gone too far. Many parents are unaware of their responsibilities for children over the age of 16 years and a public education programme on parental responsibility for older children might now be needed (Jones and Bell, 2000).

Families may not, however, be the most appropriate sources of help and complete dependence on families for support may be damaging to all parties. Young people need an alternative to family economic support and this problem could be addressed in some of the ways identified above: by improving conditions in the youth labour market, addressing the financial problems of students, and recognising young people's housing and transport costs.

Even where family support may be appropriate, there should be accessible alternatives. Schools need the resources to enable them to provide support for children during family crises such as bereavement or parental divorce. Formal information and guidance on a range of issues from sex education to labour market information should be provided for young people to supplement the informal guidance their parents may give. Community care services need to focus on the whole family and to be quick to respond to the needs of disabled and ill parents if their children are to be prevented from taking on inappropriate caring roles. Care services should provide a viable alternative to parental care for young people with disabilities, many of whom have little contact with social care agencies. Adolescent support teams could offer a short-term, sharply focused preventive service to families in crisis where problems are not entrenched. Such preventive services for teenagers should be part of a continuum of interagency family support services (Biehal *et al.*, 2000).

Joined-up policy making for young people and their families would also help (Jones and Bell, 2000). The Youth Unit recommended by the Social Exclusion Unit has now become the Children and Young People Unit and John Denham has been appointed Minister for Youth. The Ministerial Group on the Family and the Family Policy Unit, on the other hand, are based at the Home Office. The challenge for those seeking to create policies that address the problems of young people today will be to improve communication between these two policy units.

Conclusion

The last few years have seen a surge of research and policy interest in the circumstances of young people in Britain. There is a lot more to be learned about the effects of recent social change on young people and their families. The JRF will continue to support research on young people, to fill in the gaps in our knowledge about how they make the transition to adulthood, to understand the complexities of cultural variation, and to identify new policy and practice needs.

This report is titled *The Youth Divide* for a reason. Inequalities persist among young people and in some respects they have deepened. However, the polarisation described in this report hides a more complex and disturbing picture. In the social hierarchy of young people, between the 'socially included' and the 'socially excluded', there is a large (and largely invisible) group trying to survive on scarce resources, including their own resilience. The current emphasis of policy makers and indeed many researchers on the most socially excluded should be revised to consider the varying circumstances and needs of all young people. There is a danger that the proverbial iceberg will be overlooked if we focus only on the tip.

Finally, no apology is made for the obvious fact that the implementation of policies such as those suggested here will cost money. There is surely no better investment a country can make than in its own future, and that means investing in its young people.

Notes

Chapter 1

1 These inventions include Sure Start for families with pre-school children in disadvantaged areas and the newly announced Child Trust Fund.

2 Leave school, start work, save up some money, then leave home to get married and start a family.

Chapter 2

1 The NCDS and the BCS70, cohorts of young people born in 1958 and 1970 respectively, are referred to in this text as the 1958 birth cohort and the 1970 birth cohort. Each study has involved surveys of all the children born during one week in the UK, at each birth date, and longitudinal tracking over time.

2 This has implications for the system of student loans.

3 Using the YCS (1984–93) data on 16–19 year olds in England and Wales (and a follow-up sweep of 23 year olds in 1993).

4 The project was based on analysis of the JSA Claimant Survey, the Family and Working Lives Survey and the BHPS, and describes the situation in 1995, prior to the New Deal, etc.

5 A problem also encountered by the looked-after young people interviewed by Britton *et al.*, 2002.

6 A follow-up study extending the inquiry to FE is currently under way by the same team.

7 This may appear to conflict with the suggestion by Bynner *et al.* (2002, forthcoming) that the school curriculum needs to be broadened to make post-16 school relevant for those not going on to HE.

8 Around half had a paid job when at school, and some felt that their school work had suffered because of this, though they enjoyed the responsibility of working in an adult environment. The money also made them less dependent on their parents, gave them more autonomy over their own lives and gained them some respect.

9 See also Storey and Brannen (2000) on transport for young people in rural areas, and Chapter 4.

10 An earlier study (Fitzpatrick and Kennedy, 2000) found the dividing line between formal work, informal activity and criminality to be diffusely drawn among homeless people in Glasgow and Edinburgh, for whom begging and selling *The Big Issue* offered alternatives to crime.

Chapter 3

1 For young people who remain in their parental homes, there may be other ways of asserting their independence, such as by contributing board money to their parents (Jones, 1995). This seems to vary regionally. In Cambridge all but one of the parents allowed their sons to live rent-free at home, while in Sheffield young men were far more likely to be paying rent of between £10 and £25 per week, limiting their scope for spending on leisure (McDowell, 2001).

2 And suggest that state support should be provided to allow young people to remain in their parental homes should they wish to do so.

3 The JRF has funded several studies of youth homelessness in the UK (see Fitzpatrick *et al.*, 2000).

4   The study was based on interviews with disabled young people living in the parental home and in homes of their own.

5   The Social Exclusion Unit (1999a) identified poverty, low educational achievement, not being in education, training or employment, being the daughter of a teenage mother, having been in local authority care, experience of sexual abuse, mental health problems and offending as risk factors associated with teenage pregnancy. Ignorance about sex and relationships was seen as a problem to be addressed.

6   The study was based in an area of economic deprivation, where there is an extremely high rate of teenage pregnancy, and consisted of focus groups with non-pregnant young women aged 13–26, young men and some parents of teenagers. The main research involved 41 individual interviews with pregnant or ex-pregnant young women, including 11 whose pregnancies had been terminated.

Chapter 4

1   The sample consisted of 32 teenagers, 30 mothers and 31 fathers, around a third of whom were in a family relationship with one another.

2   The study was based on comparison of the 1986 and 1995 British Social Attitudes surveys.

Chapter 5

1   The Carnegie UK Initiative has a strong focus on young people's participation.

Bibliography

Allatt, P. and Yeandle, S. (1992) *Youth Unemployment and the Family: Voices of Disordered Times*. London: Routledge

Allen, I. and Bourke Dowling, S. (1999) 'Teenage mothers: decisions and outcomes', in S. MacRae (ed.) *Changing Britain: Families and Households in the 1990s*. Oxford: Oxford University Press

Barry, M. (2001) *Challenging Transitions: Young People's Views and Experiences of Growing up*. London: Joseph Rowntree Foundation and Save the Children Fund

Bell, R. and Jones, G. (2000) *Youth, Parenting and Public Policy: Chronology of Policy and Legislative Provisions*. http://www.keele.ac.uk/depts/so/research/youthchron.htm

Berthoud, R. (1999) *Young Caribbean Men and the Labour Market: A Comparison with other Ethnic Groups*. York: YPS for the Joseph Rowntree Foundation

Biehal, N., Clayden, J. and Byford, S. (2000) *Home or Away? Supporting Young People and Families*. London: National Children's Bureau

Biggart, A. and Furlong, A. (1996) 'Educating "discouraged workers": cultural diversity in the upper secondary school', *British Journal of Sociology of Education*, Vol. 17, No. 3, pp. 253–66

Bignall, T. and Butt, J. (2000) 'The views of young black disabled people on independent living', *Findings* 340. York: Joseph Rowntree Foundation

Britton, L., Chatrik, B., Coles, B., Craig, G., Hylton, C. and Mumtaz, S. (2002, forthcoming) *Missing Connexions: The Career Dynamics and Welfare Needs of Black and Minority Ethnic Young People at the Margins*. Bristol: Policy Press

Bynner, J., Joshi, H. and Tstatsas, M. (2000) *Obstacles and Opportunities on the Route to Adulthood: Evidence from Rural and Urban Britain*. London: The Smith Institute

Bynner, J., Elias, P., McKnight, A., Pan, H. and Pierre, G. (2002, forthcoming) *Changing Pathways to Employment and Independence*. York: YPS for the Joseph Rowntree Foundation

Canter, D. (unpublished) 'Going straight: transitions away from juvenile delinquency', unpublished mimeo, Liverpool University

Cartmel, F. and Furlong, A. (2000) *Youth Unemployment in Rural Areas*. Work and Opportunity Series No. 18. York: YPS for the Joseph Rowntree Foundation

Coles, B. (1997) 'Vulnerable groups', paper commissioned for JRF Consultation Meeting on proposed programme of research on young people, 14 January

Coles, B. (2000) *Joined-up Youth Research, Policy and Practice: A New Agenda for Change?* Leicester: Barnado's and Youth Work Press

Connexions (2000) *Connexions: The Best Start in Life for Every Young Person*. Nottingham: DfEE Publications. http://www.connexions.gov.uk

Dearden, C. and Becker, S. (2000) *Growing up Caring: Vulnerability and Transition to Adulthood – Young Carers' Experiences*. Leicester: Youth Work Press and the Joseph Rowntree Foundation

Dolton, P., Makepeace, G., Sutton, S. and Audas, R. (1999) *Making the Grade: Education, the Labour Market and Young People*. Work and Opportunity Series No. 15. York: YPS for the Joseph Rowntree Foundation

DSS (1999) *Opportunity for All: Tackling Poverty and Social Exclusion*. http://www.dss.gov.uk/hq/pubs/poverty

Finch, J. (1989) *Family Obligations and Social Change*. Cambridge: Polity Press

Finch, J. and Mason, J. (1993) *Negotiating Family Responsibilities*. London: Routledge

Fitzpatrick, S. and Kennedy, C. (2000) *Getting by: Begging, Rough Sleeping and* The Big Issue *in Glasgow.* Bristol: Policy Press and the Joseph Rowntree Foundation

Fitzpatrick, S., Hastings, A. and Kintrea, K. (1998) *Including Young People in Urban Regeneration: A Lot to Learn?* Bristol: Policy Press and the Joseph Rowntree Foundation

Fitzpatrick, S., Kemp, P. and Klinker, S. (2000) *Single Homelessness: An Overview of Research.* Bristol: Policy Press

Forsyth, A. and Furlong, A. (2000) *Socio-economic Disadvantage and Access to Higher Education.* Bristol: Policy Press and the Joseph Rowntree Foundation

France, A. (1998) '"Why should we care?" Young people, citizenship and questions of social responsibility', *Journal of Youth Studies*, Vol. 1, No. 1, pp. 97–111

France, A. (2000) *Youth Researching Youth: The Triumph and Success Peer Research Project.* Leicester: National Youth Agency, Youth Work Press

Gillies, V., Ribbens McCarthy, J. and Holland, J. (2001) *'Pulling Together, Pulling Apart': The Family Lives of Young People.* London: Family Policy Studies Centre and the Joseph Rowntree Foundation

Gregg, P., Harkness, S. and Machin, S. (1999) 'Child poverty and its consequences', *Findings* 389. York: Joseph Rowntree Foundation

Heath, S. and Kenyon, L. (2001) 'Young single professionals and shared household living', *Journal of Youth Studies*, Vol. 4, No. 1, pp. 83–100

Hendey, N. and Pascall, G. (2002) *Disability and Transition to Adulthood: Achieving Independent Living.* York: Pavilion Publishing and the Joseph Rowntree Foundation

Hutson, S. and Jenkins, R. (1989) *Taking the Strain: Families, Unemployment and the Transition to Adulthood.* Milton Keynes: Open University Press

Johnston, L., MacDonald, R., Mason, P., Ridley, L. and Webster, C. (2000a) *Snakes and Ladders: Young People, Transitions and Alternative Careers.* Bristol: Policy Press and the Joseph Rowntree Foundation

Johnston, L., MacDonald, R., Mason, P., Ridley, L. and Webster, C. (2000b) 'The impact of social exclusion on young people moving into adulthood', *Findings* 030. York: Joseph Rowntree Foundation

Jones, G. (1988) 'Integrating process and structure in the concept of youth', *Sociological Review*, Vol. 36, No. 4, pp. 706–31

Jones, G. (1995) *Leaving Home.* Buckingham: Open University Press

Jones, G. (1997) 'Young people and social exclusion', paper commissioned for JRF Consultation Meeting on proposed programme of research on young people, 14 January

Jones, G. (2001) 'Fitting homes? Young people's housing and household strategies in rural Scotland', *Journal of Youth Studies*, Vol. 4, No. 1, pp. 41–62

Jones, G. and Bell, R. (2000) *Balancing Acts: Youth, Parenting and Public Policy.* York: YPS for the Joseph Rowntree Foundation

Jones, G. and Martin, C.D. (1999) 'The "Young Consumer" at home: dependence, resistance and autonomy', in J. Hearn and S. Roseneil (eds) *Consuming Cultures: Power and Resistance.* Basingstoke: Macmillan

Jones, G. and Wallace, C. (1992) *Youth, Family and Citizenship.* Buckingham: Open University Press

Kirby, P. (1999) *Involving Young Researchers: How to Enable Young People to Design and Conduct Research.* York: YPS for the Joseph Rowntree Foundation

Labour Party (2001) *Ambitions for Britain: Labour's Manifesto 2001.* http://www.labour.org.uk

Langford, W., Lewis, C., Solomon, Y. and Warin, J. (2001) *Family Understandings: Closeness, Authority and Independence in Mothers, Fathers and 11–16 Year Olds.* London: Family Policy Studies Centre

Lewis, J. (1998) 'The problem of lone-mother families in twentieth-century Britain', *Journal of Social Welfare and Family Law*, Vol. 20, No. 3, pp. 251–83

Lloyd, T. (1999) 'Young men's attitudes to gender and work', *Findings* 559. York: Joseph Rowntree Foundation

Mac an Ghaill, M. (1994) *The Making of Men: Masculinities, Sexualities and Schooling.* Buckingham: Open University Press

Mac an Ghaill, M. (ed.) (1996) *Understanding Masculinities: Social Relations and Cultural Arenas.* Buckingham: Open University Press

MacDonald, R. (ed.) (1998) *Youth, the 'Underclass' and 'Social Exclusion'.* London: Routledge

McDowell, L. (2001) *Young Men Leaving School: White Working Class Masculinity.* Leicester: Youth Work Press and the Joseph Rowntree Foundation

McGlone, F., Park, A. and Smith, K. (1998) *Families and Kinship.* London: Family Policy Studies Centre and the Joseph Rowntree Foundation

MacRae, S. (ed.) (1999) *Changing Britain: Families and Households in the 1990s.* Oxford: Oxford University Press

Marshall, T.H. (1950) *Citizenship and Social Class and Other Essays.* Cambridge: Cambridge University Press

Meadows, P. (2001) *Young Men on the Margins of Work: An Overview Report.* York: York Publishing Services

Monk, S., Dunn, J., Fitzgerald, M. and Hidge, I. (1999) 'Finding work in rural areas: barriers and bridges', *Findings* 9119. York: Joseph Rowntree Foundation

Morris, J. (1999) 'Transition to adulthood for young disabled people with "complex health and support needs"', *Findings* 919. York: Joseph Rowntree Foundation

Morrow, V. (1998) *Understanding Families: Children's Perspectives.* London: National Children's Bureau

Murray, C. (1990) *The Emerging British Underclass.* Choice in Welfare Series No. 2. London: IEA Health and Welfare Unit

National Statistics (2000) *Social Focus on Young People.* London: The Stationery Office

Pavis, S., Platt, S. and Hubbard, G. (2000) *Young People in Rural Scotland: Pathways to Social Inclusion and Exclusion.* Work and Opportunity Series No. 17. York: YPS for the Joseph Rowntree Foundation

Pickford, R. (1999) *Fathers, Marriage and the Law.* London: Family Policy Studies Centre

Randall, G. and Brown, S. (1999) *Ending Exclusion: Employment and Training Schemes for Homeless Young People.* York: YPS for the Joseph Rowntree Foundation

Rugg, J. (ed.) (1999) *Young People, Housing and Social Policy.* London: Routledge

Rugg, J. and Jones, A. (1999) *Getting a Job, Finding a Home: Rural Work Transitions.* Bristol: Policy Press and the Joseph Rowntree Foundation

Shropshire, J. and Middleton, S. (1999) 'The experiences and attitudes of children from low-income families towards money', *Findings* 379. York: Joseph Rowntree Foundation.

Shucksmith, M. (2000) *Exclusive Countryside? Social Inclusion and Regeneration in Rural Areas.* York: Joseph Rowntree Foundation

Smith, J., Gilford, S. and O'Sullivan, A. (1998) *The Family Lives of Homeless Young People.* London: Family Policy Studies Centre

Social Exclusion Unit (1998a) 'What is social exclusion?' http://www.cabinet-office.gov.uk/seu/index/march

Social Exclusion Unit (1998b) *Truancy and School Exclusion.* Cm. 3957. London: The Stationery Office

Social Exclusion Unit (1998c) *Rough Sleeping.* Cm. 4008. London: The Stationery Office

Social Exclusion Unit (1999a) *Teenage Pregnancy.* Cm. 4342. London: The Stationery Office

Social Exclusion Unit (1999b) *Bridging the Gap: New Opportunities for 16–18 Year Olds not in Education, Employment or Training.* Cm. 4405. London: The Stationery Office

Social Exclusion Unit (2000) *Young People: National Strategy for Neighbourhood Renewal.* Report of Policy Action Team 12. London: The Stationery Office. http://www.cabinet-office.gov.uk/seu/publications/pat/pat12/

Speak, S., Cameron, S. and Gilroy, R. (1997) 'Young, single, non-residential fathers: their involvement in fatherhood', *Findings Social Policy Research* 137. York: Joseph Rowntree Foundation

Stafford, B., Heaver, C., Ashworth, K., Bates, C., Walker, R., McKay, S. and Trickey, H. (1999) *Work and Young Men.* Work and Opportunity Series No. 14. York: YPS for the Joseph Rowntree Foundation

Storey, P. and Brannen, J. (2000) *Young People and Transport in Rural Areas.* Leicester: National Youth Agency and the Joseph Rowntree Foundation

Tabberer, S. (2000) 'Teenage motherhood, decision-making and the transition to adulthood', *Youth and Policy*, No. 67, pp. 41–54

Tabberer, S., Hall, C., Prendergast, S. and Webster, A. (2000) *Teenage Pregnancy and Choice. Abortion or Motherhood: Influences on the Decision.* York: YPS for the Joseph Rowntree Foundation

Utting, D. (1995) *Family and Parenthood.* York: Joseph Rowntree Foundation

Walker, A. (1990) 'Blaming the victims', in C. Murray, *The Emerging British Underclass.* Choice in Welfare Series No. 2. London: IEA Health and Welfare Unit

White, C., Bruce, S. and Ritchie, J. (2000) *Young People's Politics: Political Interest and Engagement amongst 14- to 24-year-olds.* York: YPS for the Joseph Rowntree Foundation

Willis, P. (1977) *Learning to Labour.* Farnborough: Saxon House

Willis, P. (1984) 'Youth unemployment', *New Society*, 29 March, 5 April and 12 April

Appendix: The research projects

Projects commissioned in the first phase of the Young People Programme

Young people in transition
Peter Elias, John Bynner and Abigail McKnight (Warwick University and Institute of Education, 2000)

Balancing acts? Youth, parenting and public policy
Gill Jones and Robert Bell (Keele University and South Bank University)
Published as: *Balancing Acts: Youth, Parenting and Public Policy*, G. Jones and R. Bell (YPS for the Joseph Rowntree Foundation, 2000), ISBN 1 902633 48 2, £13.95 (Tel.: 01904 430033; email: orders@yps-publishing.co.uk)

Challenging transitions: young people's views and experiences of growing up
Paula Rodger (Save the Children Fund)
Published as: *Challenging Transitions: Young People's Views and Experiences of Growing up*, P. Rodger (Save the Children Fund, 2001), ISBN 1 84187 041 2, £7.50 (Tel.: 01752 202301; email: orders@plymbridge.com)

Socio-economic disadvantage and access to higher education
Alasdair Forsyth and Andy Furlong (Glasgow University)
Published as: *Socioeconomic Disadvantage and Access to Higher Education*, A. Forsyth and A. Furlong (The Policy Press/Joseph Rowntree Foundation, 2000), ISBN 1 86134 296 9, £12.95 (Tel.: 01235 465500; email: direct.orders@marston.co.uk)

Working class masculinity and the labour market
Linda McDowell (London School of Economics)
Published as: *Young Men Leaving School: White Working-class Masculinity*, L. McDowell (Youth Work Press/Joseph Rowntree Foundation, 2001), ISBN 0 86155 248 2, £12.95 (Tel.: 0116 285 3700)

Pulling together, pulling apart: The 'family lives' of young people
Jane Ribbens and Janet Holland (Oxford Brookes University and South Bank University)
Published as: *Pulling Together, Pulling Apart: The Family Lives of Young People*, V. Gillies, J. Ribbens McCarthy and J. Holland (Family Policy Studies Centre/Joseph Rowntree Foundation, 2001), ISBN 1 901455 42 4, £10.95 (Tel.: 01904 430033; email: orders@yps-publishing.co.uk)

Growing up caring. Vulnerability and transition to adulthood – young carers' experiences
Chris Dearden and Saul Becker (Loughborough University)
Published as: *Growing up Caring: Vulnerability and Transition to Adulthood – Young Carers' Experiences*, C. Dearden and S. Becker (Youth Work Press/Joseph Rowntree Foundation, 2000), ISBN 0 86155 233 4, £12.95 (Tel.: 0116 285 3700)

Young people's politics: political interest and engagement amongst 14- to 24-year-olds
Clarissa White, Sara Bruce and Jane Ritchie (National Centre for Social Research, 2000)
Published as: *Young People's Politics: Political Interest and Engagement amongst 14- to 24-year-olds*, C. White, S. Bruce and J. Ritchie (YPS for the Joseph Rowntree Foundation), ISBN 1 902633 64 4, £13.95 (Tel.: 01904 430033; email: orders@yps-publishing.co.uk)

Teenage pregnancy and choice. Abortion or motherhood: influences on the decision
Sharon Tabberer, Christine Hall, Shirley Prendergast and Andrew Webster (Social Policy Research Unit, York, and Anglia University)
Published as: *Teenage Pregnancy and Choice: Abortion or Motherhood: Influences on the Decision*, S. Tabberer, C. Hall and A. Webster (YPS for the Joseph Rowntree Foundation, 2000), ISBN 1 902633 99 7, £12.95 (Tel.: 01904 430033; email: orders@yps-publishing.co.uk)

Disability and transition to adulthood: achieving independent living
Gillian Pascall and Nicola Hendey (Nottingham University)
Published as: *Disability and Transition to Adulthood: Achieving Independent Living*, N. Hendey and G. Pascall (Pavilion Publishing and the Joseph Rowntree Foundation, 2002)

Snakes and ladders: young people, transitions and social exclusion
Les Johnston, Rob MacDonald, Paul Mason, Louise Ridley and Colin Webster (Universities of Portsmouth, Teesside and Birmingham)
Published as: *Snakes and Ladders: Young People, Transitions and Social Exclusion*, L. Johnston, R. MacDonald, P. Mason, L. Ridley and C. Webster (The Policy Press/Joseph Rowntree Foundation, 2000), ISBN 1 86134 290 X, £10.95 (Tel.: 01235 465500; email: direct.orders@marston.co.uk)

Transitions away from juvenile crime
David Canter (Liverpool University)

Involving young researchers: how to enable young people to design and conduct research
Perpetua Kirby (Save the Children)
Published as: *Involving Young Researchers: How to Enable Young People to Design and Conduct Research*, P. Kirby (YPS for the Joseph Rowntree Foundation, 1999), ISBN 1 902633 45 8, £9.95 (Tel.: 01904 430033; email: orders@yps-publishing.co.uk)
Also: *Young People as Researchers: A Learning Resource Pack* (Save the Children Fund), ISBN 1 841870 11 0, £9.95 (Tel.: 01752 202301; email: orders@plymbridge.com)

A process evaluation of the Triumph and Success Peer Research Project
Alan France (University of Sheffield) and SOVA
Published as: *Youth Researching Youth: The Triumph and Success Peer Research Project*, A. France (Youth Work Press/Joseph Rowntree Foundation, 2000), ISBN 0 86155 242 3, £12.95 (Tel.: 0116 285 3700)

Career dynamics of multiply disadvantaged 16–17 year olds
Gary Craig, Bob Coles and Balbir Chatrik (Leeds University and York University)
Published as: *Missing Connexions: The Career Dynamics and Welfare Needs of Black and Minority Ethnic Young People at the Margins*, L. Britton, B. Chatrik, B. Coles, G. Craig, C. Hylton and S. Mumtaz with P. Bivand, R. Burrows and P. Convery (The Policy Press/Joseph Rowntree Foundation, 2002), ISBN 1 86134 832 5, £12.95 (Tel.: 01235 465500; email: direct.orders@marston.co.uk)

Kinship care for vulnerable young people
Bob Broad (de Montfort University, Leicester)
Published as: *Kith and Kin: Kinship Care for Vulnerable Young People*, R. Broad, R. Hayes and C. Rushforth (National Children's Bureau/Joseph Rowntree Foundation, 2001), ISBN 1 900990 70 9, £10.95 (Tel.: 020 7843 6029; email: sales@ncb-books.org.uk)

Young women working in the sex industry (due autumn 2002)
Jennifer Pearce (Middlesex University)

Other published JRF projects referred to in this report

Home or away? Supporting young people and families
Nina Biehal, Jasmine Clayden and Sarak Byford
Published as:
Home or Away? Supporting Young People and Families, N. Biehal, J. Clayden and S. Byford (National Children's Bureau/Joseph Rowntree Foundation, 2000), ISBN 1 90099 058 X, £11.95 (Tel.: 020 7843 6029; email: sales@ncb-books.org.uk)

Action in Rural Areas research programme

Young people and transport in rural communities
Pamela Storey and Julia Brannen (Thomas Coram
Research Unit, Institute of Education)
Published as: *Young People and Transport in Rural
Areas*, P. Storey and J. Brannen (Youth Work Press/
Joseph Rowntree Foundation, 2000), ISBN 0 86155
234 2, £12.95 (Tel.: 0116 285 3700)

**Getting a job, finding a home: rural youth
transitions**
Julie Rugg and Anwen Jones (York University)
Published as: *Getting a Job, Finding a Home: Rural
Youth Transitions*, J. Rugg and A. Jones (The Policy
Press/Joseph Rowntree Foundation, 1999), ISBN
1 86134 212 8, £10.95 (Tel.: 01235 465500; email:
direct.orders@marston.co.uk)

Youth unemployment in rural areas
Fred Cartmel and Andy Furlong (Glasgow
University)
Published as: *Youth Unemployment in Rural Areas*, F.
Cartmel and A. Furlong (YPS for the Joseph
Rowntree Foundation, 2000), ISBN 1 902633 60 1,
£12.95 (Tel.: 01904 430033; email: orders@yps-
publishing.co.uk)

**Young people in rural Scotland: pathways to
social inclusion and exclusion**
Stephen Pavis, Stephen Platt and Gill Hubbard
(University of Edinburgh)
Published as: *Young People in Rural Scotland:
Pathways to Social Inclusion and Exclusion*, S. Pavis, S.
Platt and G. Hubbard (YPS for the Joseph Rowntree
Foundation, 2000), ISBN 1 902633 59 8, £12.95 (Tel.:
01904 430033; email: orders@yps-publishing.co.uk)

Work and Opportunity programme

**Making the grade: education, the labour market
and young people**
Peter Dolton, Gerry Makepeace, Sandra Hutton
and Rick Audas
Published as: *Making the Grade: Education, the Labour
Market and Young People*, P. Dolton, G. Makepeace,
S. Hutton and R. Audas (YPS for the Joseph
Rowntree Foundation, 1999), ISBN 1 902633 52 0,
£14.95 (Tel.: 01904 430033; email: orders@yps-
publishing.co.uk)

Young men, the job market and gendered work
Trefor Lloyd
Published as: *Young Men, the Job Market and
Gendered Work*, T. Lloyd (YPS for the Joseph
Rowntree Foundation, 1999), ISBN 1 902633 14 8,
£10.95 (Tel.: 01904 430033; email: orders@yps-
publishing.co.uk)

**Ending exclusion: employment and training
schemes for homeless young people**
Geoffrey Randall and Susan Brown
Published as: *Ending Exclusion: Employment and
Training Schemes for Homeless Young People*, G.
Randall and S. Brown (YPS for the Joseph Rowntree
Foundation, 1999), ISBN 1 902633 09 1, £13.95 (Tel.:
01904 430033; email: orders@yps-publishing.co.uk)

Work and young men
Bruce Stafford and Claire Heaver *et al.*
Published as: *Work and Young Men*, B. Stafford and
C. Heaver (YPS for the Joseph Rowntree
Foundation, 1999), ISBN 1 902633 19 1, £13.95 (Tel.:
01904 430033; email: orders@yps-publishing.co.uk)

**Young Caribbean men and the labour market: a
comparison with other ethnic groups**
Richard Berthoud
Published as: *Young Caribbean Men and the Labour
Market: A Comparison with Other Ethnic Groups*, R.
Berthoud (YPS for the Joseph Rowntree
Foundation, 1999), ISBN 1 899987 84 3, £14.95 (Tel.:
01904 430033; email: orders@yps-publishing.co.uk)